IN GOD'S GARDEN

IN GOD'S GARDEN

An allegorical look at church life

Don Tate

Bible references taken from The New American Standard Bible

To contact Don, email at: warvet_69@yahoo.com

For further information:
Facebook page: Donald William Tate

Book formatting by Aishah Macgill
www.finitepublishing.com

Book cover design by Steve Guest
www.sgraphics.com

ISBN 978-1-925049-14-5

CONTENTS

CHAPTER ONE

'And Jesus came up and spoke to them, saying,
'All authority has been given to Me in Heaven
and on earth.
Go therefore and make disciples of all the
nations, baptising them in the name of the
Father and the Son and the Holy Spirit,
teaching them to observe all that I commanded
you, and lo, I am with you always, even to the
end of the age."
(Matthew 28: 18-20)

A man, once, stood looking over the expanse of land that stretched before him. He stood still, and breathed deeply, as if with each breath, he was taking into himself some great energy force.

He was neither young, nor old, yet in his bearing there was youth, and in his face, wisdom beyond his years. His skin was tanned like that of a worker in the field, and there was a strength in his arms and shoulders that spoke of a preparedness for hard work.

He wore the clothes of a humble man– a gardener in fact; overalls, open-necked shirt and work boots, slightly soiled.

In his right hand he held a solid gardening fork of steel and hardwood, and under his left arm, tucked tightly against his chest, a large, well-worn, tome– *The Manual*.

It appeared to be a work of great substance and consequence.

To his right, but standing slightly behind him, stood his wife, her hand resting on the right hand of her man, together on the handle of the fork.

She was smaller than the man, yet not delicate. There was a softness about her, as there should have been, but it was not the softness of weakness. It was the softness of spirit, of compassion, and of love.

And there was also strength. In her eyes, like those of her husband's, there was a steeliness of purpose and resolve, of determination and courage. These were attributes she knew she would need in days to come.

Her female intuition told her so.

As well, her heart soared, for there was no place she would rather be, nor anybody else she would rather be with, nor any task she could envisage that could be as wonderful as that which lay before them.

It was twilight, and the dying day was before their eyes. They faced west, for that was where the sky was still lightest, and watched as the sun slid behind a low cloud-bank that girdled a turquoise, sharply-silhouetted mountain range.

As they watched, and it seemed to the couple that this was just for them, the heavens opened, and a glimpse of that eternal beauty they could only have guessed at, shone forth across the breadth of the heavens.

Before their eyes, the setting sun splashed that expanse of sky with colour and hues beyond mortal imagination and description. Glowing shades of coppers and bronzes and gold weaving in and out of wispy, radiant-white cotton-clouds. In turn, the clouds dissolved into delicate patches of pink and tangerine, trimmed with a glistening lace of platinum. Above them, remnants of rain clouds, now emptied, shone with the reflections of the fading sun– now a saffron, now a buttercup-yellow, now amber, now frosty-rose. To the north, over lavender hills, splotches of indigo and ruby curtained a pearl-blue canvas strung across a corner of the heavens. In the east, where the storm-clouds still sat hunched and bunched in spent authority, fingers of lightning speared across them, and a gloriously-perfect rainbow issued forth across the reaches of the sky. Like a giant smile, its colours starkly prominent against its ebony backdrop, the rainbow spoke to the couple who stood transfixed beneath it; spoke to their souls of a glory and a beauty beyond understanding.

They watched the display in awe, felt it purge their worldliness and sent their spirits soaring. Around them, as if cocooned for the moment, the world was quiet and at peace.

The couple smiled to each other in wonder.

The man breathed it in deeply, and smelled the lusciousness of an earth refreshed and washed clean. Then, he looked again at the land before him as it gathered in the darkness before the night, and stepped forward. In easy strides he measured out a portion of the earth, marking its length and breadth.

At the centre of the land, he called his wife to him. Together, they raised their arms to the heavens and proclaimed the land for their Master.

A last fan-spray of sun burnished the western sky, but the couple's gesture extended far beyond the glory before them.

With a gentle wind in their faces, with tears in their eyes, and with a smouldering love deep within them, the man and woman dedicated that parcel of earth to the author of the *Manual* and proclaimed the land for the Master Gardener.

'Master,' the man said, a little shyly at first, '…..Father, look upon our faces, and upon our hearts. Touch us. Let us feel Your hand upon us so that we might do that which is Your will, and do it to Your glory. Search our hearts, Master. Cleanse us of any past failure that might hinder our work. Tear it from us, so that we may be clean before Your eyes. Take away the hurts, real or imagined. Take away the fears, the weaknesses. Fill us Master. Fill us with Your love, with Your strength. And…' he added hesitantly, looking away at the land which lay before him, 'fill us with the courage to do Your work in this place.'

Then, lowering his arms and eyes, the man turned again to the centre of the land he had chosen to work.

'This earth is Yours,' he continued. 'Let me build upon it a garden that will glorify You, that will honour You, and that will please You. I ask You, Master, to bless this land, and we, your servants who will work it.'

Then, clasping his wife's hand, the two stood quietly together in the field, partakers of a heavenly calling. And for a few brief minutes, while the glory of that twilight faded, they were not on this world, nor in it, nor of it, but held tightly in the arms of the Master.

Slowly, almost imperceptibly, night fell across the land and enveloped the couple.

Chapter Two

'Sow with a view to righteousness,
Reap in accordance with kindness;
Break up your fallow ground,
For it is time to seek the Lord
Until He comes to rain righteousness on you.'
(Hosea 10: 12)

The new day dawned fresh and bright and clear.

The gardener awoke, and felt at once both physically rested, yet strangely disturbed– almost apprehensive. He had slept soundly, had even dreamed of his garden, of how beautiful and bountiful it would be in the eyes of all. He felt a strength surging within him– the strength that comes in anticipation of a heavy day's labour.

But there was something else, as well, a restlessness in his spirit which he could not account for. It troubled him. It was as if there was some doubt deep within his soul, and for a little while he wrestled with it.

But after some time in study of his *Manual*, and a period of meditation and introspection, he saw no profit in dwelling on the negative feeling, and cast it from him.

He kissed his wife warmly, and set off for the virgin garden.

He strode easily across the land with an urgency in his heart and a vitality in his soul. The early morning sun was at his back, and a zephyr caressed the land. Before too long, the early restlessness was long behind him, and again he was at peace with himself.

Soon, the area of land he had chosen lay before him.

'Master,' he whispered into the wind, 'this day is Yours. Bless me that I might do Your will, and that that which I do will be pleasing in Your sight. Thank You Master for this task which You have set before me. Grant me the strength and determination to carry it through.'

And then, standing on the thresh-hold of the land he had proclaimed for his Master, with his foot upon the heel of the fork, he added,

'For You, Lord! It begins!' And, with that, thrust his weight upon the fork and drove it into the ground.

Thus, the gardener turned the first piece of fallow ground in that place.

* * *

At the end of that day, the gardener stood in the shadows of a large tree, and looked back over the earth he had turned.

Sweat poured from his brow, his face burned from the sun, his back ached, and his muscles were tired and sore. But he thought little of his aches and pains. Instead, his eyes roamed backwards and forwards across the broken earth, and he studied the turned earth thoughtfully.

From where he stood, the earth he had broken appeared remarkably inconsistent in type, texture and colour. He looked at it anxiously. Here he had promised a garden which would glorify the Master, yet the first turning did little to encourage him.

Much of the land had never been turned before, and such soil, he knew, would present the greatest challenge, but that thought pleased him.

At the same time, there was land that *had* been turned before, perhaps by other gardeners at other times, and yet the inconsistency troubled him. Where there was lack of uniformity, a variety of gardening strategies would need to be applied to overcome it, and such procedures were known to be arduous and troublesome. But then, he thought to himself, that's what gardening is all about.

It was the universal challenge of gardeners everywhere.

Leaving the tree, he strolled back across the upturned soil. Time and time again, he stopped, and inspected handfuls of earth he scooped up in his hands. He examined each handful closely, crumbling the sods between his fingers and watching how it fell to the ground.

'Clay!' he said, in one place. 'Clay!'

He squeezed the thick, orange-coloured material in his hand, and watched it ooze between his fingers.

'You are not much use in a garden, clay,' he continued aloud, 'or to me. As you are, there is little you can do. You can produce nothing. Though there is an inherent *substance* about you, I fear you will just sit beneath the garden. You will suck out all the moisture, and all its nutrients. You will restrict root growth.'

He squeezed the clay again, felt it moulding in his grasp.

Pondering the matter further, and feeling the innate strength of the substance in his hand, he suddenly thought of the potter's wheel, and the fiery kiln, and as if inspired, suddenly saw great possibilities in the substance before him.

'And yet, your solidity may be a strength, clay,' he said, as its potential became apparent. 'But I will have to break you down, for broken you must certainly be. Else, I must dig you out altogether!'

'Yes, clay,' he continued aloud, 'there *is* potential for you after all!'

In another area, along a border region of the area he had marked as a boundary of the garden, he found the soil to be unusually dry and arid. As he turned it over, and watched it slide through the prongs of his fork, he could sense it was sour soil. There was no apparent reason for it– just a lifelessness in that particular area. It hadn't looked that way on the surface; in fact, it looked the same as the rest of the soil in the area. But exposed by the gardener's fork, turned to the light, it revealed little of substance.

'Something has poisoned you,' the gardener said aloud, a little incredulous. 'Such bitterness! Such sourness! Have you been worked too much by some other gardener? Or too little? Perhaps someone has spilled a poison on you and you have never recovered.'

He scratched his chin. 'But then again, perhaps you've never been turned to the sun before, never felt its healing balm, its very life force working on you. Perhaps you've never felt the spring rains drenching you, washing away that bitterness. Is that what it is?'

He scooped some of it up. 'Well, sour soil,' he said, 'soon I will work some fertiliser into you, some compost rich and full of essential nutrients. I'll let the sun and rain pour down upon you. For it cannot be, that one part of my garden can lie so barren!'

And he moved on.

'Sand!' he muttered in another place. Sand, he knew, was hardly suitable garden soil. To start with, it was dry and porous, and far too easily susceptible to the elements. Wind and water would slowly erode it. And there was no richness about it, no texture which could be built upon. No life-force. No fertility.

'You just lay there, sand,' the man said sadly. 'Just like the clay. The difference is, though, that you can be blown here and there by any wind, or washed away in the storms that will come, and soon you would be gone. You're not the type of soil a garden can depend upon.'

The gardener straightened his weary back, and allowed himself a smile.

'But at least you are easy to handle,' he had to admit. 'Maybe I can use you in the marshy, boggy areas of the garden to help dry them. Or mix you into the clay where your very brittleness can be of use in breaking it down.' He nodded slowly. 'Yes, I *can* use you, sand. There is value in you yet!'

And he walked on, darkness and the cool of dusk closing in on him.

In the centre of the measured area of land stood a slight crown of land, but covering a substantial area. Here the soil promised much. It was dark and heavy, rich and thick in texture. Every handful spoke of vitality and life. Here, the land received the full thrust of the sun's rays, soaked up the first rains, and because of its essential goodness would be capable of reproducing even when the seasons were not kind.

'You will provide the showpiece of my garden,' the gardener said, turning over forkfuls of the loam. 'Though you've not produced yet, you shall produce the fairest blooms. The centrepiece of my garden you shall be.' And then, as an afterthought, 'And some of you I will spread across other areas of the garden. Such healthy soil in just one place would be to deny your value to the entire garden.'

Wearily now, he moved on, his fork across his shoulder. Soon, he came upon another area of soil not unlike that in the crown. It too, was healthy in appearance. He stopped, and examined it curiously, for he recalled that as he had laboured in turning it, this area of soil had produced a myriad of odd, deformed plants, and weeds. And yet it looked so rich on the surface.

'Such richness!' the gardener said aloud. 'Why is it that no plants of quality have grown here?'

He was puzzled by the irony.

'Can you be *so* rich, soil, that you will support any growth, any plant at all, yet none of any substance? How can this be? Would you raise up both weeds *and* healthy plants? Would I need to be always in this part of the garden rooting out plants of little consequence so that the healthy ones would prosper?'

The gardener knew he would need to consult his *Manual* about this soil. Such a paradox, he thought.

But already a germ of an idea was forming in his mind, and he let it develop.

He could sense some divine inspiration, as if the Master was there with him, leading him on.

'Yes, I know what I can do with you! I can mix you with that sour soil lying over there, and through such a mix perhaps the true potential of each of the types can be realised. The sour soil will take from you, and you will give it willingly because that is the nature of your type of soil. And, at the same time, the sour soil might help you appreciate your worth all the more, because *it* has nothing to give. Yes,' he added, 'you might yet prove to be my best soil. I can spread you throughout the garden, anywhere and everywhere, and wherever you settle you will boost that particular area.'

He smiled to himself, blessed at the revelation.

In another place, he cried, 'Rocks! Rocks! And more rocks!'

With a hint of anger, he threw them from him.

'What can I do here?' he cried aloud. 'Fields full of stones and rocks will not support plant life. Their roots will not penetrate you. And it will take a long time for the sun and rain to break you down. And time in a garden is of utmost importance.'

His face furrowed a little, and then a smile broke across his face.

'But then again, perhaps there can be a use for you too! I can use you to hold my garden together in the areas where storms might wash the soil away. Maybe down near the brook over there, where it looks like floodwaters could easily break the banks.'

One by one, he lifted the rocks and stones of the field to examine them. There was no beauty in them, just a roughness, all jagged edges and harshness. But it was their weight and solidity that spoke to him.

'Yes, even *you* rocks can be of use to me. On your own, you may yield little, but it may very well be that *you* will be the strength that binds my garden. With careful placement and rendering, I can also use you as retaining walls and foundations for more elevated gardens in time. And, in doing so, even you will be broken down to a point where I can use you even more effectively and productively.'

Almost in darkness now, in yet another place, the gardener found an area where his fork had barely scraped the surface. Once, he had thought his fork might snap as he laboured to turn it. Scooping away what loose earth he could, the gardener found that large roots held the soil firmly in its grasp. The tree that they had nourished had long since died, and its remains were now part of the earth. It was as if they were saying, 'We served one master. No other will grow in its place!'

But the gardener knew about such roots. Gardeners the world over found them to be a source of stubborn resistance to change, even hostile towards it.

'You *will* come out, roots!' he said, allowing a righteous anger in his voice. 'Even if I have to burn you out, out you will come! But first, I will bring the axe, and the mattock! You will not hold onto this soil and resist a new work in this place!'

There was a fierce determination in his words.

And by then, twilight had fallen, and a darkness began to pervade the land gain. The gardener walked from the earth with his fork over his shoulder.

As best he could, the soil had been worked over and the garden was ready. Ground that had lain fallow for so long, had at least, at last, been broken.

If nothing else, the gardener knew he had made a start on his enterprise. It was a start as bold and honest as he was capable of, and he allowed himself a smile of satisfaction at his effort. There had been gardens he was aware of in which the soil had never been completely turned even once, and which produced little in the way of any plant of quality as a consequence.

And without any trace of smugness or pretension, the man believed he had set a standard he knew his Master would be proud of.

'There is still much to be done,' he said to himself. 'It will need to be turned once again, and yet again if necessary, to yield a harvest of the quality the Master would desire of me. And tomorrow, I will bring the tools to do so.'

Turning home, the man again placed the fork over his shoulder, and as he walked, he gave his Master thanks once more for the weary bones and the soiled hands, and the opportunity he had been given.

Chapter Three

*'And He gave some as apostles, and some as
prophets, and some as evangelists, and some as
pastors and teachers,
for the equipping of the saints for the
work of service, to the building up of the
body of Christ.'*
(Ephesians 4: 11-12)

In the days that followed, a sense of satisfaction overwhelmed the gardener and his wife. They knew that there was something essentially right about the direction in which their lives were headed, and about how they were setting about the task before them.

Each day the man rose early, even before the sun crept its way over the low hills that rolled away towards the east.

He would slip quickly from his bed and don his working clothes, eager to be at his work. And each day the anticipation of hard, physical work was quickened to his soul, and the strength that he required flooded into the very marrow of his bones.

These were the days of passion, of single-mindedness, of vision, and of true love for the task he had undertaken.

In these early days, without fail each morning, he would consult his *Manual* before setting off to his garden. This was essential, because within its pages he knew were the keys of totally successful gardening, indeed, the keys to a personal appreciation of the very nature and meaning of life itself.

Without the *Manual*, or without a true understanding of the principles it proclaimed, gardening, was of no consequence.

At the same time, it was not a work that could be easily digested.

Much of it was written in obscure gardening jargon, as if it's author was requiring of His reader a certain diligence and perseverance in deciphering it. In other places, it was written in purely scientific terms so difficult to comprehend that it threatened to always remain beyond the understanding of the gardener. Or there were parts so expressive, so poetic, so profoundly rich in instruction that it challenged the very essence of the man's intelligence.

It was at once simple, yet ambiguous, superficial yet profound, full of terrors and yet, full of love and joy.

The gardener and his wife knew that it was their task to unlock its secrets and pass it on in the establishment of their garden. No way else could gardeners, or even the garden itself ever reach its full potential unless they were prepared to search the *Manual* for its deepest secrets and truths.

It was a mystery they both understood. Especially the man. For it had been he who had first felt the call to gardening.

Years previously, before the *Manual* had held any significance in his life, and when gardening was an occupation he sneered at and looked upon with loathing, a stranger had crossed his path.

That stranger, a passionate, wild-eyed man, had spoken with great conviction about the condition of all plants in general, and about gardening in particular. He impressed upon the man a sense of gravity about the condition of plant life in general, and their imminent mortality. Although not a true gardener himself (in truth, he had no gardener's heart, just a desire to stir other men's souls to the profession) the stranger spoke in explicit terms about the consequences of plants left to fend for themselves without the care and guidance of a gardener.

As he had left, the stranger had handed the man a large book.

It was weighty, an imposing *'Manual'* that appeared to be about plants, and their growth. But it was much more than that, the stranger promised. It also contained the secrets of successful gardening–instructions and precepts whereby those with a heart for gardening could grow plants of such superior quality as to dull the blooms of the most exotic plant growing wild. It was a *Manual* that contained assurances of technique, whereby plants, suitably tended, would grow with a majesty beyond the normal range of experience.

'All the great questions of plant-life are answered in this *Manual*,' the stranger said, standing on the doorstep, 'the secrets, the truths, the answers. And it is written with such an authority that it challenges the heart of every man who would read it. One cannot help but be uplifted and inspired and challenged. Its words eat into the very marrow of any man of substance.'

'But I've read such *Manual*s before,' the man had said, although a little weakly, because the truth was, his search for a meaning to his life had been only a haphazard, superficial process. 'I've searched for a reason for life, a purpose, but all the great *Manual*s I've come across about life appear to be contradictory.'

The stranger had looked him in the eye with such intensity it threatened to burn through him. It spoke of a driving determination that appreciated the man's very real dilemma– the dilemma of all men, world-wide who aspired to truths about where they lay in the greater, eternal scheme of things.

'This *Manual* makes many promises,' the stranger said. 'But none more profound than this, *Search and you will find.*'

The stranger's eyes glowed with fire. 'It is but one truth. There are so many others. But in essence, in this *Manual* you will find the truth about plant life, its purpose and reason. Just as simple mathematics are accepted without question, a study of this *Manual* will leave you in no doubt. You will instinctively know that what it promises, to be true. Step by step, precept by precept, the fundamental truths about the very existence of plants are spelled out. It highlights the truths about life itself, and our responsibilities. Search it. If you are an honest man who desperately seeks answers, you will find within its pages the answer to every question you ever asked. If you have a gardener's heart, you will be inspired by it, and desire to share it. Such a man would find gardening to be a calling.'

Then, the stranger had turned and left abruptly, saying he had no time to tarry over-long, for there was much he had to do elsewhere, so many more men of good heart he had yet to reach.

So the man had read the gardening *Manual*, along with his wife. And they found that what the stranger had said was most certainly true. It was at once both condemning, yet enlightening. It spoke of death and disease, yet was inspiring, and insightful, and contained revelation of the most profound kind.

Out of that, on a balmy spring evening years ago, both had felt called to raise a garden as a life's work.

And, over time, both came to the conclusion that the *Manual* would be their sole source of inspiration and guidance, and that constant reference to it, and reliance upon it, should be fundamental to the rest of their lives as gardeners.

* * *

Despite the desire of his heart and the eagerness to please his Master, the reality was that the work in the garden was physically demanding, never-ending, and full of challenge and disappointment.

And the gardener's strength was limited by his own humanity.

At the close of each day, the gardener would wearily make his way home, and after the evening meal soon be fast asleep. It would usually be the sleep of a man of the fields– deep and wholesome.

But often, when he awoke, there was a weariness in his bones that remained. In that state, often the words of the *Manual* were lost to him. He read it, of course, even believed he was still studying it, but at times the commitment to concentrate was not there.

'Husband,' said his wife one day, 'perhaps you must take more time off from your work so that your study of the *Manual* and your personal appreciation of its Author, are not jeopardised.'

'We must work as long as it is day,' he replied. 'There is much to be done, and we must work until it *is* done.'

Gently, his wife put her arm on his shoulder. 'But husband,' she started, hesitant so as not to provoke, 'if we have the wrong emphasis in our lives, one or the other will suffer. It's a question of balance.'

'There comes a time,' he replied, 'when one must have an imbalance, even if it is only for a short time. The truth is, if I don't stay out in the garden, we risk losing what we have established. There are all sorts of dangers out there waiting to devour what we have cultivated. As much as I hate to admit it, there are other gardeners out there lacking integrity who would pluck out my best plants in the dead of night and steal them. Others would come by and under the pretence of brotherly love look at our plants with envy. Some have been known to pretend admiration for what we are achieving, pretend an affectation for our plants, then surreptitiously pour out poison on to them. I must remain vigilant, even if there is a short-term cost.'

The wife did not respond. She knew that there was truth in what he said. She also knew that many gardens eventually failed when the work itself assumed priority over study of the *Manual*.

It was a common dilemma for gardeners worldwide. And all she could do, she realised, was to re-double her own efforts to compensate for her husband's laxity.

That, she had determined, at the start of their enterprise, was to be her role– to be behind the scenes perhaps, yet still be the backbone of it.

So, as the days went by and turned into weeks, then months, and without the gardener ever really realising it, he began to take the *Manual* for granted. In-depth study gave way to superficial reading, and then to lip-service of it.

Over time, its essential importance to his work became obscured.

But worse, time-poor as he found himself, and exacerbated by the effort required and the demands expected of him as the problems of building a new garden became more apparent, even his vision for the garden became blurred.

Eventually, he would pay dearly for his failure to reconcile the need for strict adherence to gardening principles, and the actual working out of them. It was an error of judgement arising out of good intentions– yet the *Manual* had contained clear warnings about such error, so he would have no one to blame, but himself.

*   *   *

But there came a time when the garden truly looked like a garden. The fine work he was doing was becoming obvious to those who resided in the general vicinity, and passers-by, as well as other gardeners had watched it take shape with mixed feelings.

There were those in the area who preferred not to even have another garden in their midst, seeing them only as places that lured men and women from the more acceptable pursuits of work and play. Such people looked upon gardeners as essentially lazy, unproductive, and even exploitive, and their produce of little interest in the wider affairs of men.

Gardeners were used to such criticism. It had always been the case.

The fact was, gardens in any community always provoked reaction. By their very nature, the presence of a garden full of quality plants challenged plants that grew wild or roamed free in the countryside. Any plant could not help but be challenged by the garden variety plant. It was as if they prodded the conscience, demanding of all others that they search their hearts for the true meaning of life– or to account for how they spent their lives, and to wonder about what lay beyond their earthly journey.

Strangely, many plants outside the garden preferred not to dwell on such things, seeing such concerns more as a condemnation of the way they spent their lives. Many such plants prioritised the now, rather than the future, and felt that gardens were an intrusion to be barely tolerated in their midst.

In truth, while they were forced to accept that gardens had a basic right to exist amongst them, many plants looked upon them with disdain. Yes, sure they looked nice and smelled good, and by their presence appeared to lift the overall quality of all plants in the most positive of ways, but they also seemed to provoke unnecessary friction. Families of plants were often torn asunder, split this way and that, a grafting taken here and a grafting there.

As well, as their opponents often pointed out with smugness, there were even petty animosities between the various gardeners which often spilled over into the community in acrimonious debate, resulting in bitter resentments and division.

Quite often, the cause of such disputation lay in the hearts of the various gardeners involved. It was quite obvious to many, that some gardeners seemed to set themselves apart as individuals, professing that *their* work was of greater significance than another's, that *theirs* was the more noble calling, that *they* had greater talent or insight, and as such demanded of people a respect and appreciation not necessarily earned.

Unfortunately, the wider community came to view gardeners as superficial and hypocritical. With good reason in many instances, gardeners became equated with shiny-haired, snake-oil salesmen prepared to hoodwink, swindle, lie and cheat their way to prominence.

And once they had a garden of their own, they invariably were revealed as weak-willed men of little consequence, who relied on a coterie of stronger individuals to do most of the work in the garden.

The disintegration of gardens worldwide was a phenomenon, and as a consequence, there was a tendency towards scepticism of all gardeners.

Not that this *should* have reflected on the gardens themselves.

But because of gardeners whose gardening techniques were blatantly superficial and transparent, the very essence of gardening as an alternative pursuit was lost on the great majority of observers.

While gardens should have been perceived as havens– a respite from the daily pressures of life, and as a source of inspiration, most saw them only as pretentious small businesses managed by men with limited intellect or ability, and regarded their enterprises as being of no great benefit.

Rather than being seen as places of great influence on the gentler nature of man, and rather than being a place that provided a peace and contentment beyond their wildest imaginings, gardens were too often seen as a wasteland of gross, artificial trees, and plastic plants. In fact, more often than not, such places were widely regarded as the last bastion of hypocrisy, and downright embarrassing to be seen in, or involved with.

That is not to say that the public perception of gardens and gardeners was necessarily accurate.

In fact, many gardeners went about their business blissfully unaware of how the wider community felt, and could care less anyway. To some, their gardens, regardless of its size or its condition, was an all-consuming passion that fed their egos and satisfied temporal ambition. As long as they were satisfied with their own sense of importance and the job they were doing, that was all that mattered.

But a new gardener, and a new garden in their midst– *that* was reason for concern and interest! And many had mixed feelings about the intruder, and how it would affect them.

Some were delighted, coming from the old school that followed the *Manual's* demand to take the gardening message into all corners of the earth. They saw the new garden through eyes unclouded by personal ambition, delighted that a grander vision than theirs was being countenanced and pursued.

Such men believed that new gardening blood produced keen competition to grow plants of finer quality– something that would elevate the public perception of all gardens.

Others though, perceived that a new garden was a threat to theirs, especially when they noted the keen preparations of the new gardener, and the general health and vibrancy of the garden. This type of gardener not only saw the gardener as a threat to their very existence, but a risk that the plants they had raised might be regarded as being inferior and flawed in comparison with those produced by the new methods being adopted, and in such a comparison they too would be seen as the failures they really were.

It boiled down to the question of what sort of quality were the plants in the garden, and what techniques were employed in the particular gardening process.

Would the new gardener grow his own plants, or would he plunder other gardens? Would he raise up a brand of plants that had some peculiarity that might reflect poorly on all plants? Would he introduce diseases or blight into the community that could condemn all plants? Would he blend into the existing gardening sub-culture, or operate outside it? Would his methods lead them all into ridicule?

And so on.

Such questions were of great concern to many gardeners whose livelihoods often depended upon the relative size and health of their gardens. Anything that threatened either, was potentially devastating.

For such men, what might once have been a grand vision, had given way to pragmatism.

But none of this really concerned our gardener and his wife who, led by their hearts, were shaping a garden to please a greater Power than any other which existed in the community.

But unbeknown to them, there *was* a force of some magnitude working both within, and without, the garden, as indeed it was in *all* gardens. It was a force with one objective– to destroy all gardens and the plants therein.

It was loosed by the arch enemy of all gardeners, was fuelled by ignorance, and was to manifest itself in this particular garden by the subtlest of means.

*   *   *

At a certain point, the couple were pleased with the progress they had made. Although it proved to be a slow process, they knew that thorough preparation, and deliberate attention to every facet of gardening was the key to success.

They had learned this secret through careful observation of other gardens they had visited, or studied, and which had ultimately failed. Such observation had been a fundamental aspect of their own personal preparation. They knew there were lessons to be learned.

For example, it was a fact that for a time, many gardens looked healthy, and their plants were often highly regarded, and prized. But when difficult times came (frosts, pestilences and the like) these plants often lost their fine outward appearance. Superficially, they might have looked good, but lacked substantial root systems and their demise was slow.

Sometimes a gardener would simply lose interest and let his garden deteriorate without ever really noticing it was. Plants would wither and die (unless keener gardeners plucked them out and saved them, or stole them as noted earlier. Less scrupulous gardeners were often accused of doing such a thing, even though it may have been done with the best intentions).

Occasionally, such gardens ceased to exist. They were either so neglected, or so devoid of plants, that they could no longer even claim to be true gardens.

But our gardener, in this instance, was a resolute man who had studied hard before embarking on the undertaking, and he determined to work steadfastly to produce a garden and plants of real quality. Anything less was not worthy of such an effort.

'It will *not* happen to *my* garden,' said the man to the very earth itself. 'This ground *will* be broken up. I will turn it to the sun and rain as often as I must to ensure it is properly prepared, for that which I intend to sow is precious.'

It was this resolve that fuelled his muscles and strengthened his arms as he toiled at his work.

* * *

By now, the gardener was also using other tools for the work, for the fork had done its job. It had broken the soil– that had been the first step. Now it was the turn of the shovel, the axe, and the mattock.

With the shovel, he turned great clods of soil, driving it deep into the dark earth, then turning it over. With quick, clean thrusts of its blade, he cut the clods apart till they lay shattered and exposed to the sun.

Backwards and forwards he worked across the land, turning and breaking, turning and breaking.

Sometimes he would stop, and turning those soils he knew to be inferior, carried them to other areas of the garden and spread them. Then he would return with a shovelful of richer earth to replace what he had taken.

Where there were rocks, he brought out his mattock. Digging deeply around them, he would lever them out and carry them off to places where they would be of more use.

'A most useful tool, the mattock,' he mused to himself, on one occasion. 'With your sharp end I can strike and shatter the rocks. And with your broad blade I can get under them, and around them, and dig them out, for out they must come!' Yes, he concluded, the mattock was a most useful tool, though not favoured by all gardeners, for its use required a raw strength and a strong arm, and many fellow gardeners were weaklings at heart.

Roots though, were a different proposition. For these, the gardener brought down his axe. Broad-bladed and double-edged, the tool did not fail its user.

Swung from high above his head, the gardener crashed it down upon the largest roots, smiling to himself as it sliced clean through them. Over and over again, the axe would descend in mighty arcs into the roots, its blade flashing and glinting in the reflection of the sun. With each blow, the gardener would feel his muscles ripple along his arms and into his back and shoulders. He could feel the strength of his body growing with each blow he delivered.

He was a man, and wielding the axe was a man's job. It was not for the faint-hearted or the weak of spirit, for the job required of such a tool was strenuous and demanding. He had known of some gardeners who were reluctant to use the axe, leaving it to the wife or an underling.

Such men were beneath contempt, he thought.

Paradoxically, the harder he worked, instead of tiredness, his strength was continually renewed, and invigorated. It was his belief that there was nothing like hard, physical work to stimulate the very essence of man, and it was an ethic he held dear.

Surely, he thought, no garden could be properly prepared without an axe to cut out the roots of old trees and stumps. And yet, he realised, looking at the blade of the axe as he rested at one time, without *my* strength, without *my* actually picking it up and swinging it, it would lay useless. It was a profound thought, he realised, and he marvelled at the simple truth it revealed.

'So many tools at my disposal,' he mused, 'and all of them useless without *my* arm, and *my* desire and *my* intent.'

It did not occur to him, despite his study of the *Manual,* to appreciate that without an even greater sense of purpose and direction guiding him, he and the tools would both have had limited success.

* * *

It was on one late, Spring afternoon, almost before the man himself even realised it, that he stood on the high ground of his garden and knew that his preparations for building the garden had been completed.

Before him, in all directions, the ground was broken and turned, exposed to the full richness of the sun and the rains which would come in full measure during the Summer. The evenness of texture he had desired, had been realised. Rocks had been removed, or relocated, and roots had been either torn out or cut to levels that would not affect plant growth.

His garden was ready for sowing, and planting.

For a long while, with his wife at his side, the gardener stood looking over the land that represented their life's work, and for which the Master Gardener would ultimately judge them.

'It is done,' he said, and her eyes smiled back at him. 'Let us give thanks.' And where they stood, they gave the Master Gardener thanks for His strength, and for His provisions, for they knew His hand had indeed been upon them.

CHAPTER FOUR

'There is an appointed time for everything.
And there is a time for every event under heaven–
a time to give birth, and a time to die;
a time to plant, and a time to uproot
what is planted;
a time to kill, and a time to heal;
a time to tear down, and a time to build up;'
(Ecclesiastes 3: 1-3)

With the ploughing done, the time for planting had come.

The gardener did not rush the task, even though he already knew in his mind his design for the garden, as well as its arrangement and the combination of plants he desired.

He led his wife around the broken ground and showed her how it would be. This was right and proper. She was his partner after all, and should know the plans and directions he had for their garden.

'There,' he said, pointing to a particular spot, 'will be the centrepiece of our garden. In it, I will place those trees and shrubs that will prove to be most stable and hardy, for it is them that must shade those not yet used to the full glare of the summer's sun. And it is those whose roots will bind our garden. They will be the very foundation of our garden– its strength.'

His wife nodded approvingly.

'Perhaps they will not be the most attractive plants,' she added, 'but I see what you mean. A garden needs strong trees with straight, solid trunks. Plants of permanence. In those we will have power and continuity.'

'And around them,' continued the man, his eyes aglow with the pleasure of seeing a vision about to come to fruition, 'I will plant bushes and shrubs of great beauty– plants that will bloom in the soil and the sun, and whose flowers will always bear testimony to their general well-being.'

'And to the care of their gardener,' suggested his wife, smiling gently. Intuitively she knew that the health of a plant often depended not only on its positioning within the garden, but the gardener's own particular care of it.

It was stated so in the *Manual*. So in her heart, she knew it to be the truth.

'They will get that,' her husband replied. 'To plant a garden is to know that. It is a life's work.' But there was no unkindness in his reply.

He took her by the hand to where an old tree stood in the garden.

'I could not remove it,' he said. It is a cedar–very old, well-established, and healthy. I believe it was meant to stand here. Beneath it I can plant young, immature trees that can be sheltered and protected by it, and all the time they'll gain in vigour and vitality. In those young trees, the future of our garden can be assured.'

'And will there be a place for flowers?' asked the wife, knowing that there would be, but eager to see where they would be planted. These would be her special joy. Too often she had seen other gardeners disregard flowers for the sake of more trees and shrubs. Many gardeners, she knew, held flowers in scant regard.

'Yes. Yes– in a special place,' her husband replied. 'Over here, beside this brook where birds will flock at dawn and dusk, their sounds echoing across the valley. It is the perfect place for flowers.'

He was aware of the delicate nature of flowers, their fragility, and their sensitivity. There was gentleness, and understanding in his voice.

His wife agreed. With the waters of the brook whispering along its pebbled route, and a patch of soft grass and mosses and clover beside it, the setting was perfect, and her spirit whelmed up within her.

'It is perfect,' she said. 'Perfect for flowers to bloom.'

Flowers were her personal concern. So often disregarded as mere adornments, it was her philosophy that the merest of flowers was just as important in the overall scheme of things as the most majestic tree.

Here, she thought, the flowers will be far enough away from other plants that often stole the limelight in most gardens. Perhaps here, flowers, and not trees or shrubs, might assume some prominence.

'And I see you've built a rock wall to protect them,' she said.

'Yes, flowers need a little more protection,' the man replied.

He was well aware of their special qualities. He had seen flowers that should have grown to be magnificent specimens, end up dwarfed and stunted because trees and shrubs in close proximity had been allowed to grow unchecked, or unpruned. Too often, their growth had been restricted by the failure of gardeners to hold them in any real regard, too often they were left to grow as best they could without the care they needed.

More often than not, flowers were grown in areas of a garden with little prominence or significance. But then again, the gardener was also aware of instances where flowers had bloomed mightily, despite scant attention, then appeared to lord it over others of its type almost in spite. They were the exception rather than the rule though. Gardeners, generally speaking, saw little financial benefit in flowers, nor did they attract visitors like the more magnificent trees had a tendency to do.

In truth, in most gardens the blooms of flowers had to struggle to be seen beneath the unsightly, wayward shrubs that made up the bulk of most gardens.

'Flowers are meant to bloom here,' he added, and he felt he really meant it.

In a smaller, raised bed of rocky soil, the gardener spread his arms out wide.

'Cacti!' he said. 'And plants with spikes and thorns. This will be a special place for plants like these. While they will get full sun, the soil is not too rich, and the bed is well-drained. That's what they like most. And there is plenty of room for them to grow.'

'You know that other gardeners don't want them in their gardens,' the wife said.

It was more a statement of fact, rather than a question.

Plants that other gardeners had difficulty with had always intrigued her. How a true gardener could just ignore, or discard, plants that had difficulty growing, seemed to go against all notions of true gardening, in *her* opinion.

It warmed her heart to know that her husband shared her concern, and she squeezed his hand warmly.

'Yes, I know that,' he answered. They *are* difficult to grow. And sometimes they can get out of hand and spoil a garden. And I know they are difficult to tend and prune,' he added, smiling. 'They are difficult plants. But what sort of gardener would I be to leave them out? There must be a place in our garden for every plant, beautiful or ugly, for the straight of limb and the twisted, for those that grow with little care and for those that faint in the slightest change of weather. I know that some will prick me as I care for them, wife,' he said, 'and some won't respond at all. But there must be a place for them all regardless. The *Manual* has made that quite clear. Gardeners who restrict the plant types they will keep in their gardens not only do a disservice to plants generally, but limit their own capacities to grow as gardeners.'

Simplified gardening, it was called. Or specialised gardening. Gardening made easy. For some gardeners, raising only a limited type of plant made the task so much easier. They required the most basic of gardening regimes, and still afforded the gardener the mantle of respectability that came with the job.

Our gardener though, was a different breed of man.

'A garden of easy-to-grow plants will be a superficial garden, and its gardener a failure,' he continued. 'Anyone can tend a garden filled with healthy plants– but much, much more is expected from one who is truly called to carry out this task. We must maintain a broad vision, prepared to grow all types of plant, without fear or favour.'

'And isn't it true that some of the most beautiful blooms are found on plants that are ugly in appearance,' the wife added. It was an aspect of gardening that gave her an added sense of excitement. 'It's amazing, isn't it? Often the most flamboyant tree or shrub produces the dullest bloom, and the plants that are least in appearance, so often trampled upon and overlooked, are the ones that reveal the rarest flower, the most delicate and perfect of blooms.'

He listened intently, and knew she was speaking the truth.

'And the most beautiful perfume,' he added, as they moved on.

After they walked in silence a little while, she suddenly stopped him, and holding his hand tightly, asked a question that had been on the very tip of her tongue for some time.

'Husband, I have heard you talk mostly of trees and shrubs, and of places where flowers and difficult plants may be tended, she said, 'but now I must ask you this,' and her voice wavered a little, 'how much of our garden will be devoted to the planting of seeds, to new life which we have sown ourselves and can watch grow as our very own? Will there be room for them?'

She asked it deliberately, for she knew the *Manual* made it quite clear that the establishment of new growth from seed was the primary task of all gardeners. From seeds would appear plants already rooted in the bed in which they would grow. These would be plants that would not be damaged in any transplanting process. Plants that would not have been exposed to any poisons or chemicals used in other gardens. Plants that would not bring in any blight or diseases that often ran rampant in lesser gardens prepared by men of little quality.

She was aware that this was the case in the majority of gardens. She had read of plants that had suffered badly at the hands of poor gardeners, and even when rescued and transplanted into a relatively healthier garden, never reproduced or reached full bloom. And she had seen for herself plants whose outward appearance was one of lush growth, but whose root systems were bound up, or so diseased that they were all but dead. Appearances, she knew, could often be deceptive.

The gardener looked his wife squarely in the eyes.

'Wife,' he said, and it was all he could do to hold back the tears, 'this is a new garden. New plants. New beginnings. Fresh seed, and fresh seedlings. Seeds we will sow ourselves. Acres of them, right across that whole section of the garden,' he continued, pointing to a wide, flat area of broken earth. 'It is our main task, I agree. And there is much to be done in that field.'

Then he flung his arms out wide in an expression of joy.

'What a garden this will be! But wife,' he said, in a cautious tone, 'before we plant seed we must have trees and shrubs of various height and at different stages of growth so that we can protect the new seedlings from the wind, and to shade them in summer, and to provide warmth during the cold winters. And we must plant other types of trees as well,' he added, his enthusiasm bubbling over, 'I must make room for the cast-offs from other gardens– the neglected, the broken, the spoiled. That is what a garden is for, and what makes a garden. Could I *only* have a garden of brand new plants I had raised myself? How boring that would be? And how risky? In a poor season I could lose them all at once. And think of the work it would take to tend only baby plants. I would be forever in the garden.'

She looked at him. Would that be so wrong, she wondered, to have to *always* be in the garden? But she said nothing.

'But fresh seed,' he continued softly. 'Young healthy plants from seed we sowed ourselves! That will be our private joy! And the Master's as well, for surely that is at the heart of the very matter.'

She squeezed his hand, and let her concern go. In that firm grasp she knew her man was a gardener who would do the Master proud. And her.

CHAPTER FIVE

'For even as the body is one and yet has many members, and all the members of the body, though they are many, are one body, so also is Christ.'
(1 Corinthians 12:12)

And so, in due course, according to plans and a design of his own choosing, but led by the greater spirit behind the enterprise, the gardener planted his garden out. It was an on-going process that took place, day in, day out, year in and year out.

Slowly it took shape– the old and the new, side by side. His garden was a combination of extraordinary character and diversity.

Some, the couple planted themselves, but mostly the plants that appeared in the garden came from a variety of sources, and in ways and means that often bemused them.

Along with the cedar (which was the dominant feature) other trees were now in place. There were trees that seemed to appear as if by divine intervention, and suddenly just appeared. There were trees he procured simply by visiting other gardens, and by his very presence secured them. Some were given willingly by other gardeners keen to help another garden grow. Others were given with more sinister motives behind the gesture– invariably they had some problem the other gardener hadn't been able to deal with. Sometimes he found himself lifting out a neglected plant from another garden for fear it would die, and transplanted it into his own.

Occasionally (and to be honest, this pricked at his conscience) he often visited such gardens with a view to taking cuttings he later propagated himself, but although somewhat of a dubious activity, he glossed over it, given his bolder vision for his garden.

Even in gardening, there were grey areas, he conceded, grey areas he could find no adequate answer for in the *Manual*. On such questions, the *Manual* only tantalising referred to them as being beyond the 'comprehension' of normal men, that there would be a time when all questions would be answered.

That would be the time, the gardener thought, whenever his conscience bothered him about a particular act, or course of action.

And then there were plants he found that other gardeners had thrown out– ugly, twisted plants diseased or damaged, and left to die along narrow roadsides. Or plants that just grew unwanted in the unlikeliest of places and often too bothersome for other gardeners to worry about collecting. Plants that clung precariously to life in the most unlikely of places, barely rooted on rock ledges, gasping for life in a wasteland, or drowning in murky waters at a swamp's edge.

In *his* garden, our gardener had decreed, there had to be room for all types of plants.

And so it transpired.

While the cedar was quite a dominant tree in the landscape of the garden, other fine trees and shrubs had established well, and they complimented each other, each in their own way.

A terebinth was the gardener's favourite. It was a slender tree but had large, thick foliage, and reproduced faster than any other plant in his garden. It had an area to itself in the garden, and beneath it the gardener placed plants that grew quickly in the same soil that the terebinth favoured— rich, and well-drained. Plants like azaleas and tulips.

In various places, he had transplanted oak trees. Now they were growing, full-bodied and solid, and since they were evergreen, always looked spectacular. Around the oaks, the gardener had placed the smaller, more fragrant shrubs like the hyssop and the spike.

In the orchards, fig and pomegranate trees shadowed the grapevines and gourd trees, while palms and almond trees complimented their area with a contrast of size, and height, and shape of canopy.

In time, the garden bloomed with a wondrous selection of plants and such variety and colour and shape it was a wondrous thing.

Down by the brook, willows stood in weeping thickets as if to guard the papyrus and canes that lined the banks. Here, the woman had planted her beds of crocus, chrysanthemum, and anemone; in another place, wild-blue hyacinth and lilies draped into the water alongside wormwood and gall.

What might have appeared an incongruous and even foolish blend of plants and colours to men of lesser vision, worked in this garden. It was a splendid panorama of rich diversity.

But it was in the fields of newly-sown seed that the gardener often stood with the greatest sense of accomplishment. These were the wider tracts of land where he had hand-sowed seed– the hardest option of all, but one that fulfilled an innate desire within him as it did with all true gardeners with the right heart. If there was ever a true sense of purpose, in the hand-sowing of seed it was richly revealed.

The wife, too, watched those open fields with particular concern. She had watched her husband sow the fields as farmers had done since time immemorial– the grain held in a measure over the left shoulder, and scattered with the right hand. She had watched the endless toiling, his broad back often almost yielding beneath the weight as he criss-crossed those open tracts, and her heart had soared with pride at his efforts.

And almost as she held her breath, beneath the large tracts of fertile ground, fresh seeds were breaking from kernels, thrusting upward into the dark and the cold to that wonderful, mystical world of life above. It was a sight that sent her spirits soaring.

*   *   *

In the fields, the crops of barley and wheat stood like a massed brown army beneath the sun, reaching higher and higher towards it. All under the gardener's watchful eye.

But overall, the centre-piece, and major attraction, was the raised area. Here, the sweet-scented white flowers and fragrant leaves of the myrtle swept over the firs and pines and sycamores. These were the focal point of this part of the garden– beautiful trees of varying shape and size, each significant in its own right, each serving a purpose of its own, and each contributing to the total effect. Beneath them, the frankincense gum and the myrrh shrub exuded fragrances that seemed to uplift the taller trees, and at the same time ministered to the ailments of the gardener and his wife.

And the seasons came and went, year in, and year out.

*   *   *

In Spring, the rains would come and pour out their nutrients over the garden.

Time and time again, the clouds would roll in over the western skies like a great, grey blanket and sweep across the earth. When the rains left, the plants would stand fresh and anew, and the soils would be softened and enriched by a life-blood planned before time itself– drenched with a dew from heaven.

The Spring rains never ceased to amaze the gardener.

Often he would stand out in the rains himself, and let it flow over him as well. Afterwards, he too, would feel cleansed and renewed. His spirit would be invigorated, and the whole world would smell fresh and clear, and a vitality would shine within him, and flow through to the plants in his garden. It was as if he imparted to them some mystical strength, and he being nothing more than a link in some wonderful design he could only guess at.

But what he *was* acutely aware of, was that the rains meant life, and when it rained on his garden, it flourished. It was a ritual of great and singular importance.

So too, with mulching.

If there was one truism that applied to gardening, it referred to mulching of plants. Simply, any gardener worth his salt loved to mulch

Mulching was a most important aspect of gardening, and the gardener was resolute in his application of it. He spent much time in the collection of it, and great consideration in the placement of it. Indeed, when it came to caring of plants, nothing raised his spirit more than the process and consequences of mulching.

It had many benefits, both in the presentation of the garden, and the general well-being of all the plants in it.

In the first place, it was important because it not only protected the nutrients in the soil around each plant, it kept the weeds at bay. Weeds detracted from the soil and were apt to proliferate, so keeping them to an absolute minimum in a garden bed was essential. It also prevented the soil from drying out, and the richness within the soil from leaching out. And because of the very essence of its nature, over time, it broke down and enriched the very soil itself, and in time, became one with the very marrow of the plant.

In every garden, it was a truism that the quality of plants raised was directly proportional to the gardener's propensity to apply mulch.

More importantly, in Spring, and into the early Summer months, the gardener also applied liberal amounts of fertiliser.

This was a most difficult exercise, involving complex needs, measures and reactions. He used a wide variety of types and blends, in essence, not so rich as to burn, but rich enough to impart strength and power to the root systems of the plants.

Fertilising was very important, and the gardener knew it. Across the garden he worked, working the fertiliser in around the plants, or under the soil, and sometimes (in diluted form), *over* the plants if he felt such radical treatment was called for.

All the time, he took the utmost care— especially with the roots.

Roots, he knew, were the plant's life-line, and to disturb them, even in the application of fertiliser, was to jeopardise the very existence of the plant.

'A most interesting substance, fertiliser,' he exclaimed suddenly, one day, as his wife joined him for lunch. 'Every plant needs it, but each reacts to it in different ways.'

They were sitting beneath the sycamore, the fragrances of the garden wafting over them. She loved to hear him talk about gardening, no matter which aspect of it they discussed. There was vitality in such discussion, she believed, out of which came validation and reinforcement of their ideals.

'Look at our cedar and myrtle. Look at those shrubs over there,' he said, pointing. 'See their foliage? Look at how green it is, how rich and shiny, how full of life. Look at the sturdiness of their trunks and boughs. It's as if they have absorbed so much fertiliser, it's stored within them. It's almost like they live only for constant fertilising.'

'Or none at all,' said his wife. 'Perhaps they are as healthy as they can get, and you're only wasting time and effort on applying more. Surely there comes a time when a plant must survive, and reproduce, of its own desire to do so.'

'All trees need fertiliser,' the gardener replied. 'No matter how old or mature. Right up until they die, they can exact something worthwhile from fertiliser, provided it's the right mix. I believe most gardeners agree on this.'

'You don't think there's a point they reach where fertiliser becomes irrelevant? A point where they've done all the growing they're going to do?'

'No,' he replied, firmly. 'Who can pinpoint such a time? Who's not to say that they have only reached a certain height stage of growth because of the energising properties of constant fertilising? If I stopped the process now, I would never be sure they reached their maximum growth, their true potential. How can such things be judged?'

She nodded in agreement. It was a reasonable point.

'But *these* trees,' he continued, pointing to a windbreak of willows sheltering the brook, 'I've got to be careful with them. They seem to get all they need from the soil itself, and I often feel I *do* waste my fertiliser on them.'

'Then you contradict yourself,' she said.

'Not at all,' he replied. 'There *are* plants that are fertilised from within, as if they find what they need from the soil, or sun, or air. I just don't need to be concerned about them. They exist side by side with other trees, but never rise to any great heights. Yet they are just as important in the overall make-up of the garden.'

It was a paradox, he knew, and although it needed further elaboration, he didn't pursue it. The physical work was hard enough without taxing the intellect as well.

'What about our new seedlings? How much do they get?' she asked, not wishing to push the point. Invariably, he was mostly right in technique, she had learned. While her knowledge was essentially intellectual, his was grounded in the practicalities.

'Very little,' he answered. 'I just make sure there's enough in the soil, or around them to satisfy their most basic needs when they will require it. Too much fertiliser, applied too early, often impedes their growth. Sometimes it kills them outright. I like them to appreciate the wonder of new life. Let them breathe in the sun and the air. There's plenty of time later to apply fertiliser. And the rain washes a little over them anyway.'

'Is it the same for all new plants?'

'Well, it's interesting,' he said. 'I actually learned by trial and error. It depends on the plants themselves. Sometimes they die right off. Or they grow stunted, or twisted into weird shapes as if the fertiliser directly affects their root systems. Or they grow furiously for a time, then suddenly the fertiliser is exhausted, and the plant is left with luxurious growth, but roots that are shallow and weak. It's as if the energy within fertiliser goes directly into growth, but as you know, growth without firm rooting is potentially disastrous.'

'So fertilising is important?' the wife asked, idly. She already knew it was.

'Very much so,' he replied. 'Very much so.'

It was a subject he loved to discuss. To fertilise, or not to fertilise? How often? How much? They were questions not even the *Manual* was completely clear about, leaving such decisions to the competence of the gardener. It was almost as if by such testing, the true worth of gardeners could be defined.

Yet it was such a complex issue.

Sometimes the gardener would hear of great results being obtained by other gardeners using vastly different blends of fertiliser. Often it would only be a new mix of the same basic components all gardeners used, and the only reason it was proving to be more successful lay in the method of application, rather than in the properties of the fertiliser itself.

Occasionally, a gardener would stumble onto a formula that achieved spectacular results, usually the result of painstaking research of the finer points of gardening in the *Manual*. Such gardeners would proclaim their revolutionary new technique as a 'revelation', and expect to be held in high regard by their peers as a result.

The gardener was not adverse to the borrowing of other gardener's research. In fact, he felt it was to his credit that he did so, and revealed a certain humility he was secretly proud of. But it showed wisdom, he believed, and he knew of many gardeners who lacked it.

These were men who managed little plots with smaller visions, who refused to accept that other gardeners had anything at all to offer. Instead of being alert to new trends or discoveries, they kept to their own counsel and the tried and proven methods. As a consequence, their gardens grew few plants of prominence, and were generally profitless enterprises to be sneered at by those who knew their way around the gardening world.

It was a special pride that some gardeners had– that they alone had all the answers to successful gardening. Such gardeners never experienced explosions of growth within their gardens, nor did they raise plants of the size and general good health of wiser men. They were not men destined to have gardens of prominence within a community, nor any sense of personal accomplishment.

Curiously though, such men would still hold onto their gardens with a fanatical zeal, because losing them was a failure of immense proportions with eternal consequences. Such men were aware that their care of plants, indeed the individual growth of every plant in their gardens, was a matter for which they would ultimately be held responsible for, and accountable for.

For those who had made the effort to find out, the *Manual* outlined these principles quite clearly.

*   *   *

So it came to pass, that over time, a great and wonderful new garden stood established within the community. And it flourished.

And all the while the wife gave thanks for what she and her husband had been given, and for the energy and enthusiasm granted them to carry it out. The gardener gave thanks when he could, or when time permitted, or when his energies allowed.

CHAPTER SIX

'Already he who reaps is receiving wages,
and is gathering fruit for life eternal;
that he who sows and he who reaps
may rejoice together.'

(John 4: 36)

Seasons came and went, and everywhere the gardener looked, consolidation was taking place. From the myrtles and cedars to the spreading shrubs, from the new growth to the grafted, the garden spoke of a vigorous and healthy state.

Looking out over the garden with his wife one Summer afternoon, the gardener expressed his pride in what they had achieved for the very first time.

'We have planted, and raised, a beautiful garden,' he said. 'It is the finest garden I have ever seen.'

'We have been blessed,' replied his wife. 'Our hard work has borne fruit.'

'Yet there is still much to do,' said the husband with a sigh. 'The task is a demanding one.'

'We always knew it would be,' she said, squeezing his callused, work-hardened hand. 'That was part of the commission. There can be no turning back. It was never a task for the weak-hearted.'

The gardener sighed again. It was a long and drawn-out sigh. 'But there's just so much of it to do,' he said. 'And the peculiar thing is, the more time I spend in the garden, the more the garden seems to need me in it!'

It was something that had gnawed at him for some time.

Although the garden was largely self-sufficient now, and provided for the gardener and his wife as much as they provided for it, the harder the couple worked, the faster the garden grew and needed re-shaping.

It was a never-ending task. New combinations. New designs. New plantings. And always, a rooting out of the dead, the cutting off of broken branches and dead wood, or the working over of the soil around the under-productive plants. It was a constant effort, never-ending, back-breaking labour that had broken many a man previously.

At the same time, the garden had reached a point where it had become financially viable and afforded the gardener and his wife a comfortable, if not too affluent, lifestyle. This had never been a paramount concern, but it was a truism that the labourer must still be paid. Outside the gardens, it was an issue other professionals sneered at.

'Fancy getting paid to sit around with plants all week,' they'd say. 'What an easy life!'

Gardeners didn't argue the point. It was an argument they couldn't win. Outsiders had no comprehension of the rules that governed gardening, no understanding of the complexities of the issues required or the efforts entailed, or of the greater consequences of the gardener's efforts, and to argue the case with non-gardeners wasn't worth the effort. Nor was it any of their concern, gardeners rationalised. If the garden was producing dividends, all the better, because it meant the gardener had been doing something right.

Nevertheless, the fact remained, the task *was* a wearying one, and the gardener felt it more than his wife did simply because it was the strength of *his* arm that sustained it.

Occasionally, both would stand and look back over what they had accomplished, and both would be filled with feelings they knew were best kept to themselves.

Pride had been the downfall of many a gardener they had come to know, and the *Manual* warned that it was an emotion to be restrained lest it should lead to a fall. It was common knowledge that when gardeners began to dwell on their personal accomplishments and not give due praise and thanks to the source of the inspiration, or even acknowledge the *Manual's* influence, it usually marked the beginning of the end of them as successful gardeners.

Which was not to ignore the fact that a beautiful garden had certainly been established by the couple.

And it was a garden that was arousing much interest across the land, not only because of its size, but because of its variety of plants, its wonderful appearance, and the overall effectiveness of it within the community.

It was a garden that other gardeners were beginning to watch intently, with interest, and some with barely-disguised envy.

The gardener found the reaction of other gardeners a little difficult to understand. They would make polite visits and hold polite conversations, but all the time their eyes took in all facets of the garden, and generally their jealousy and envy turned to open hostility and cold contempt.

Some had attempted to steal some of the more prominent plants. Others had dropped a little poison here and there as they walked through the garden. Some had offered hints and advice of a dubious nature, while others found opportunity to criticise.

'Your plants seem to lack that personal touch!' one said. 'You don't spend enough time with them, talking to them, tending them individually.'

'You bother with them too much,' said another. 'Give them too much time and they'll wear you out. You *do* have a life of your own, you know.'

'Too much water!' said another. 'You're drowning them! They'll rot in the ground! Let them find sustenance for themselves. It promotes a deeper root-system.'

'Your plants are mostly root-bound,' said another authority. 'Perhaps the ground is still fallow.

You've got a lot more work to do if you want plants of real quality. And let's make this clear. After all, the quality of your garden is a reflection of you and your wife. That's how the gardening community judges you, you know.'

'All show, and no fruit!' from yet another, known for the manifestation of fruit in his smaller, more isolated garden. To this particular gardener's way of thinking, unless a plant was actually the finest of specimen and always in full bloom, it was of no consequence.

Unfortunately, such plants could only bear fruit for a particular time, and when they stopped, he disregarded them in favour of those who could. He saw no difficulty in managing his garden in that manner, believing that such productivity was not only a reflection of his own abilities as a gardener, but what the *Manual* actually demanded.

Others criticised the use of fertiliser, the profusion of flowers (at the expense of sturdier fruit-bearing shrubs) the positioning of various plants on the overall design of the garden, and so on.

And in that criticism by his peers, there was such isolation and rejection, it confounded him. Such reactions were indeed curious, the gardener often thought to himself.

Personally, he preferred not to comment on other gardeners or the quality of their gardens, though he was not unaware of what was happening around him. He simply believed there was no positive outcome from such negativity, and preferred to rise above it.

But he was troubled at the inconsistency of the calling of gardeners.

Since all gardeners had apparently accepted the great commission to save plants, and establishing gardens was a good way of doing so in an organised manner, some gardeners appeared to pay only lip-service to it after getting started. Often, such gardeners tended gardens either totally bereft of plants of quality, or kept plants so badly treated so as to be only shallow echoes of their true potential, or allowed their gardens to be so overrun by weeds and noxious plants that they were a disgrace in the community, and detracted from the image of all gardeners.

The gardener had little time for men such as these. He and his wife had not accepted their commission lightly. They knew what was expected of them, felt it in the depths of their spirit.

They were not about to be put off by the petty jealousies of gardeners more concerned with worldly ambition than saving dying plants. Or by gardeners unable to properly tend those they did have.

At the same time, the gardener took care not to condemn those same men for their lack of vision and purpose. That was their business, he concluded, and the right of another far greater than he to judge them.

He only knew that this garden was his responsibility, and that he too would also be accountable for how he worked it. The *Manual* was vague on the matter, but most experts agreed that a great judgement would be made on gardeners as to how they tended their gardens, and their plants, and the accountability would be severe.

Many a gardener who had damaged plant life, either accidentally or deliberately for motives known only to them, had paid dearly as a consequence, or watched as an almost divine retribution was carried out in one form or another.

He had known of gardeners who had toiled with all honesty for many a long year, then, after a simple error of judgement, lost all.

Till that accountability was asked of him, the gardener was determined to tend his garden as best as he humanly could, for as long as it took, and regardless of the extent of its demands. It was an aspect the gardener often raised with his wife when the couple found some spare time to share with each other.

'It's the way of it,' said his wife. 'To be productive, a garden must be continually worked at.'

'Yes, I know these things,' replied the gardener. 'But the peculiar thing is, and this annoys me the most, I seem to be spending most of my time with the trees and plants I had hoped would require the least of my time.'

'I have seen that,' said his wife, nodding. It was a fault she had noticed, but she had held her tongue. There were times, she knew, when her man must see his errors for himself, in his own time.

'Yes, it has bothered me for some time,' he continued. 'I placed those larger trees and shrubs in the crown, in the most prominent positions, so as to be the focal points of the garden. They were placed there to attract the eyes of the public, and to stimulate growth of plants by shading and protecting the less vigorous ones that surround them.'

'And...?'

'Well,' he said, shaking his head a little, 'it's a curious thing. They do what I expect of them to some extent. They look fine, give the appearance that they are nothing less than the finest specimens, but it seems that every time I enter the garden I must attend to one of them for some reason or other. Perhaps it's a broken branch here, or some deadwood that needs to be removed there, or even having to lift a drooping bloom to the sun. Always there is some little task that needs to be done. I had hoped they would require little effort on my behalf, since they were already strong when I planted them. But it hasn't been the case.'

'Are other parts of the garden suffering as a result?'

'Not to any great extent, I think,' he replied. 'I've tried to make sure they don't. That's why I spend such long hours out there. I try my best to look after them all.'

The wife was silent for a time. Then she reached for his hand.

'Yet some are,' she said hesitantly.

The gardener was surprised. 'Which ones?' he asked.

'Well my flower beds for one,' she said gently. 'Would you look at them?' She had been hoping for such an opportunity.

'Let me see them then,' he said, setting off across the garden. And then he added, 'Are they getting enough water and fertiliser?'

'Yes. They get both,' she answered, 'though to be honest most of it only comes in a diluted form, as run-off from your larger, raised areas where you seem to concentrate it. The flowers themselves get very little direct coverage.'

It was a mild rebuke, said gently, and lovingly. She was careful not to be critical.

As soon as the gardener saw them, he knew that his wife had spoken accurately.

'Perhaps I have been remiss here,' he agreed, fondling the dry, lifeless leaves of one flower, and casting his expert eye over others.

For a while he stood looking over the dry flower beds, and gazing up at the strands of fine trees and rows of healthy shrubs that covered the gentle hillsides. His appreciative eye and instinctive feel for such things meant he could assess the situation accurately, and he realised he had been remiss here.

'I may have spent too much time looking after my larger plants, 'but...,' he added, almost as an afterthought, 'you must remember that it is those larger plants that make our garden what it is. In them there is strength and solidity.'

'And what is a garden without flowers?' she asked hesitantly.

'I know what you're thinking,' he said. 'But without the larger trees and shrubs our garden would attract little interest. It would be bare and uninteresting. It would be unattractive. It is these plants that reach higher, and bloom more boldly than others. It is these that attract birds and insects and bees which assist in the fertilisation of all plants.'

Asserting herself, the gardener's wife knew such thinking must not go unchallenged. Yet she was also aware of her role, and her place.

'But they do not make a garden on their own, husband,' she countered. 'Flowers are just as important. In fact their blooms are as highly regarded as the least of our plants in the eyes of He whom we set out to toil for. As you know, when He walked in His garden, flowers ministered to Him more than any other plant. They were a special blessing. And much honoured.'

Now she grew bolder.

'And who may judge the relative qualities of growth and bloom anyway? Is the bloom of a tiny flower less significant than that of the tallest tree? Where in the *Manual* does it state that size, or prominence, dictates the worth of a bloom? Such a thing is not for us to judge. The merit of a bloom is not decided upon on the basis of size, but whether or not it reaches its true potential– whether or not it rises to those levels only a greater judge than me knows it has.'

The gardener pondered her words. Usually he paid only lip-service to what she said, since it had largely been *his* sweat, and *his* vision that had created the garden. To a great extent, her contribution had passed him by. In truth, he rarely acknowledged her earnest and wholehearted support, because she did it mostly out of his sight, and felt no need to remind him so.

But this time her words hit home.

'Flowers are just as important in a garden as any other plant,' she added, getting back to her original concern.'

It was true, the gardener conceded to himself. He had never intended to dispute that fact with her. A garden without flowers was simply not a garden. But he also knew of gardens where *only* flowers grew, and they were just as sorrowful a sight as gardens where flowers were peripheral concerns. There had to be a balance, he knew, and he had tried to establish such a balance in *this* garden.

He went through the garden beds, examining the flowers carefully.

'They aren't dying,' he concluded, almost triumphantly. 'There is some life in them.'

'But they are far from healthy,' she replied. 'It's as if they are lacking something. Some of them never flower at all, and those that do are as bland and colourless as any flower I've ever seen.'

'Then let's plant some roses amongst them,' the gardener said.'Roses! Why roses?' his wife asked.

'And lilies-of-the-field. And narcissi,' he continued. 'but roses, first of all.'

'Why?' she asked again.

'Because roses grow tall and majestic,' he answered. They will grow beautifully in any type of soil. They don't need the same care as most other flowers do. It's like an in-built thing within them. They can grow with little effort from gardeners. And they can provide us with the contrast of colour we need to counter the fine blooms produced by the plants in the major areas.'

'And the narcissi?' she asked.

'Again, it's a curious thing about flowers. I've noted it in other gardens. Put some beautiful flowers in a bed of average-looking flowers, and those of the lesser variety seem to respond remarkably. It's as if the beauty of such flowers inspires the rest to reach up and grow in a way they have never done before.'

'Narcissi will do this?' she asked.

The gardener nodded, seeing the new plants in his mind. 'At the very least,' he mused, 'their perfume will fill the air and enrich the whole garden.'

'And will you use such flowers, husband?'

It was not an idle question. Again, it was one she had to ask. Too often she had seen beautiful flowers of all varieties bloom in other gardens, only to be left to die and wither on the stem. She knew such flowers, once neglected, rarely ever reached the same heights of beauty ever again. Nor did they bloom as profusely.

'When the flowers are ready, certainly,' he said, 'for flowers turn the heads of all.'

He moved to her and put a hand on his wife's shoulder. 'And they will be *your* responsibility, wife,' he said gently. 'You best understand them, and appreciate them. I will leave it to you to advise me how best they can be used. The responsibility is yours.'

'No,' she said, firmly. 'The responsibility is yours. The *Manual* has made it quite clear how flowers are to be used to best advantage. And *you* are the gardener. It is *you* who must answer for how you use them, and for all that takes place in this garden.'

She kissed him softly.

'But I will do what I can. Assist you as best as I possibly can.' *That*, she had come to realise, was *her* life's work.

CHAPTER SEVEN

'Therefore, my beloved brethren, be steadfast,
immovable, always abounding in the work of
the Lord, knowing that your toil is not in vain
in the Lord.'

(1 Cor 15:58)

Consolidation of the garden was a never-ending, on-going process which required total concentration of the gardener's energies.

Now, with seed planted for a new season, with special grafting cut and rooted in places of permanence, and with the majority of other plants achieving wonderful levels of growth, the gardener and his wife turned to another task dear to their hearts– the collection of plants no other gardeners wanted.

In most instances, other gardeners deliberately shied away from those types of plants for they were types that promised little, and generally detracted from the aesthetic appearance of a garden. They were often as difficult to have in a garden as young, immature plants were. But whereas the young plants grew wildly with the sheer enthusiasm of being reborn, the wildness in rejected plants was a manifestation of such rejection.

For these plants were a type not only rejected by gardeners, but by most members of the public who preferred to see them on rubbish piles than in garden beds.

But *this* gardener, with the true soul of a gardener and not the wishy-washy superficiality of so many other gardeners he knew about, truly believed that for a garden to be complete in every sense of the word, it must cater for all types of plants. Fine looking plants in a garden were evidence of good gardening skills to a certain extent, but the acceptance and treatment of previously rejected plants reflected the true gardening heart and spirit as the *Manual* clearly demanded.

So it was that the gardener and his wife spent long nights scouring the countryside for those plants no other gardener really wanted.

They found them in the lowest of places and in all states of disrepair and ill-health. Plants so neglected they were but bare, leafless stalks. Plants that had been trodden upon and broken so many times that they lay almost lifeless on the ground. Some had been torn from places of security and left to rot on public compost heaps where only a tentative root kept them alive. Some they found had been burned and disfigured, both by gardeners who had sprayed them carelessly with strange chemicals, and by the world at large which had damaged them by various acts of cruelty.

The couple collected such plants from many places. From tiny patches of soil on barren rock faces where the cold and the heat had tortured them day and night; from cold, dank caves where the sun had never reached; from lonely, inhospitable places where love was neither given nor known; and from the garbage tips and compost heaps of a community that saw little value in them.

They gathered them in, the gardener and his wife. Plants so ugly, so twisted, so deformed, stunted, sick, and weary that it took all the compassion and will-power available in the couple to even reach out to them, let alone carry them back to their beautiful garden.

But once there, they were placed carefully in the garden, each in a special place. Some needed the protection of established plants, a careful blend of soil to nourish roots unused to such richness, and, at the same time, a location where they could receive full sun and rain in rich measure.

These plants were a special delight for the gardener, almost as important as those plants he had raised from seeds he had sown himself. To turn such sorrowful plants into healthy ones that would contribute to the attractions of the garden was a source of personal enrichment for him. Not only was it an integral part of their commission as gardeners, but their heart's desire. To save those that had been lost, and to restore those that had been sick– this was as much a responsibility of the role of gardener as was tending the wholesome plants.

Whether or not they contributed to the overall aesthetic appeal of the garden was irrelevant. It was enough to know that he had provided a garden for them in which there was an opportunity for new life.

How they responded was very much up to the individual plant itself. He could only do what he could, and leave it to those greater forces that operated on his garden to do the rest.

*　　*　　*

Consolidation also brought with it many extra demands on the gardener's time, and energies.

Caught up completely in the maelstrom of gardening activities, a less-than-desirable influence was being exerted upon the gardener over which he had lost control, even if he had known of the danger. Unfortunately, he didn't.

His study of the *Manual* had fallen away almost completely, and personal communion with his own source of inspiration now faltered.

He had not desired that such a thing would happen, for both activities were vital aspects of his life and chosen profession. Good gardening required good health, and good health required the feeding of not only the physical man, but that spiritual component as well. Oversight had become laxity. And laxity had become habit.

On many days the gardener returned from the garden bloodied and wearied with bruises, welts and raw wounds.

It was the plants themselves that did most damage to him. Often they would strike his face, or prick his body as he tended them. Plants with spikes and thorns scratched him. Falling branches or bark, and even the nuts of certain trees would hit him. Or he would stub his toe on roots exposed by drenching summer storms. What he gave to his garden in love, he received back with cuts and bruises.

And there was no respite from it, for while the nature of the work might have changed, it was still tough work.

Expansion and shaping were now replaced by maintenance of that which had already been established.

Often he was wearied to his very soul, and only the gentle personal ministry of his wife carried him on. Time and time again, she bandaged his wounds with salves and ointments from the garden itself, as was her role, and took upon herself the weighty tasks of faithful communion and the study of the *Manual*.

And while that was good, it was not enough to sustain either the man, or herself.

Or the garden.

CHAPTER EIGHT

'And do not fear those who kill the body,
but are unable to kill the soul;
but rather fear Him who is able to destroy
both soul and body in hell.'

(Matthew 10: 28)

One morning, as the first breaths of yet another Winter whispered across the land, the gardener woke with a heaviness of heart and spirit he could not account for.

Unable to shake the feeling, he decided upon an early morning stroll through his garden. The light of a new day streaked across the heavens breathing a freshness into the world, and the gardener sucked it in deeply. It was cool and soothing, yet the depression weighed upon him still.

The garden was still and quiet. Where sunlight met the silver dew, the ground shimmered like a blanket of diamonds. It was so beautiful, the gardener thought. It occurred to him that he spent so much time actually working in the garden, creating and nurturing, that he actually had little time to sit back and really appreciate the aesthetics of what he had created.

He walked among the plants, and though he guarded himself against it, he found it difficult to hold back the pride that surged within him. A mixture of fragrances, and splashes of colour delighted his senses.

It *was* something to be proud of, for these were plants and trees and shrubs that *he* had planted and nurtured. Plants he had watched grow from seeds that he had sown himself were now firmly established in prominent places, part of his solid foundation process. Rows and rows of flowers and vegetables sparkled with the dew, and over there, fruit trees of all varieties hung heavy with fine fruits. Yes, he thought, it was very hard *not* to be proud of a job well done.

Thus it was that morning, and the gardener in a self-congratulatory frame of mind, that he chanced upon a tree dying in his garden– his favourite terebinth tree. And it was as if his world crashed around him instantly.

He knew immediately that it was dying, although at this point there were no obvious signs. It was more a matter of a gardener's sixth sense at work about plants they cared for– an instinctive, intuitive feeling that only the very best gardeners developed. Suddenly he felt his very soul ice over.

'Not this tree!' he cried aloud. 'Not this tree!'

It was almost a prayer, but even as he uttered it there was an instant conviction that he had surrendered any right to request divine assistance. He had been remiss in the area of thanks for a very long time now, and knew immediately that any right to ask for help was negated.

It was a revelation of profound significance.

He walked to the tree tentatively. Anxiously, he looked for a reason– some evidence to support the feeling that something was terribly wrong here. For this was no ordinary tree.

The terebinth had been planted first in the garden, all that time ago when the garden was all but bare. He had placed it in a special position, away from the elevated area reserved for the evergreens, but on a hill nevertheless, so it had a certain prominence.

This was a tree that not only *looked* good, but *was* good. It was as tall and straight and strong of limb as the finest of any tree in the centre area, yet it spread a canopy of foliage far richer and deeper and thicker than any other.

And, more importantly, it reproduced! Often! Season after season, new seedlings appeared around it– seedlings which the gardener carefully dug out and transplanted throughout the garden. It was something the far more attractive trees rarely did, and it was why the gardener needed it in his garden; the type of tree every gardener tried to pray into his garden.

Eventually he found what he was looking for in the heart of the terebinth's trunk, just under its first spread of limbs– a thick, grey substance that seeped from its smooth surface. The gardener had never seen such a sinister-looking sap, and he knew as he looked at it and felt its deathly-ooze, that it was a terminal.

The reality of it struck him to the very marrow of his gardener's soul.

Hurrying home, he searched his *Manual* with a new diligence and zest. He had neglected it often during the long days of establishing the garden, and the realisation of such an error was immediately obvious as he scanned its pages for help. In it, somewhere he knew was the cure for every disease known to gardeners about diseased plants– but it was knowledge that required diligent study and research.

Some of the measures were obvious, and he tried them all.

First, he washed and cleansed the wound itself with oils and disinfectants. But they provided only superficial healing, and in no way reached the heart of the disease.

A tree bandage proved equally ineffective.

Extra doses of water and fertiliser had a more curious effect. After the application of both, the tree seemed to regress visibly, as if to totally reject such pathetically-human attempts to heal it. It was as if the tree itself mocked him.

Day by day the gardener watched the tree wither visibly. Soon all its foliage dropped away, and a sickly paleness came over its boughs, and there seemed a weariness in all its limbs.

The gardener watched it die with a heavy heart, and with the frustration of a man who knew he should have been able to prevent the loss. He knew he should have had a cure– the *Manual* itself assured him of it– and he knew it was every gardener's responsibility to be able to locate and apply it. And he knew that the key to saving the tree lay within himself.

Somehow, he realised, it was *his* actions, or *his* neglect, or *his* carelessness that was responsible for the impending death of his favourite tree.

Desperately he sought outside help, consulting fellow gardeners, even calling down some of the leading horticulturists in the land. No one was able to help.

His fellow gardeners reacted in a variety of interesting ways. While they too had suffered similar losses at some time, they had accepted such deaths as a sad, but natural, part of the gardening process. They could not sympathise with the gardener's distress, and found it an embarrassment in fact. Just part of the natural order of things, they said.

Other gardeners secretly delighted in his loss, since his garden far outshone theirs in size and shape. And still other gardeners caused him more anxiety than comfort, because in diagnosing the disease, they began to question every aspect of the gardener's techniques. In fact, some even openly criticised some of his methods he had employed in the establishment of the garden.

Reflecting upon this later, the gardener realised that such comments were born out of malice and envy, and from thinly-disguised jealousy, and he shook them from his soul.

As for the horticulturists, that brand of man who had once been gardeners themselves but who had since moved on to loftier, more supervisory capacities, they offered only perfunctory solutions, and were generally critical of the gardener's methods as well.

'Gardeners must ultimately be held responsible for the health of every plant in the garden,' they told him repeatedly. 'Every gardener is responsible for the total health of every plant in every respect. If you call yourself a gardener, you should have the knowledge to be able to treat every disease. If you haven't, you don't belong in the profession.'

The gardener listened with a growing anger to the negative comments heaped upon him. He *had* prepared his garden well. He *was* conversant with the *Manual's* instructions on gardening. He *had* tried everything he knew to save his tree.

Yet, deep within him, there was that niggling, personal accusation that somehow he *was* at fault.

Or was it in his wife's eyes that he saw it?

She said nothing. She helped all she could, and supported all his attempts to save the tree as best she could. But in her heart, she knew it was a vain exercise.

And she too, felt the loss terribly, if not more than her husband, since her motivations and integrity had never wavered.

* * *

The tree died while the gardener watched on helplessly.

When it was over, and he had checked it for any last-minute regeneration as the *Manual* suggested was a possibility, he cut it down with furious blows of his axe, both in rage and an inner agony. Then he dug out its stump and roots, and burned it in the one day.

He cried then, as it burned, and in the flames he thought he saw an odd thing, his own reflection. It was a spectre, dancing in the flames, taunting him, laughing at him.

His wife, who had watched and tended the whole garden while her husband had fought to save the tree, came to him as the tree burned into the night.

'You did all you could, husband,' she said. 'Now you must put it behind you. You must replace it, and reshape the garden. Rebuild it.' She spoke to him gently, her hand lightly on his head as he stared into the flames.

'That tree *was* my garden– our garden,' he answered. 'It was the most beautiful tree. It wasn't like all the others. It reproduced easily. Not many of the others do to the same extent. They should– I've cared for them as best as I can, and they do occasionally drop a seed here or there– but mostly they seem to just grow bigger and brighter. It's as if their capacity to regenerate is consumed within themselves, with their own growth.

'But the terebinth wasn't like the others. Its growth seemed to match its ability to reproduce. With each new seedling it dropped, I sensed it grew even stronger within itself.'

'You can replace it,' she said simply.

'It would not be the same,' the gardener replied. 'I planted that tree with my own hands. I nursed it through the frosts of winter and the droughts of summer when we could so easily have lost it. I trained it to grow straight, cut and pruned it, and now....'

'And now it's gone,' his wife persisted. 'You still have a beautiful garden. We have much to be grateful for. And you can, no...you *must* raise up another like the terebinth we've lost. After all, that's what gardening is all about.'

But the question haunted the gardener. 'But why *that* tree?'

The wife pondered it for a while as they sat quietly. Then she spoke, carefully choosing her words.

'Why not? Does there have to be an answer? All things must die eventually. Perhaps, simply, it was that tree's turn to die.'

'But it was still young, still strong and healthy. It was a tree in its prime,' he said, in a manner that irked his wife. It was something of a self-pitying cry, and she felt he was above such carrying-on.

'There is a time to live and a time to die. The *Manual* tells us so,' she answered. 'And when it's time to die, it's time to die. Who are we to question that? There is a greater Power than us that does not think as we do. All we can do is accept the way of things, and learn from them. We have been given a test.'

'And we have failed,' said the man, miserably.

'No,' she replied, 'perhaps we have just been found wanting in some respect,' the wife continued, now with a certain sharpness in her voice. It depressed her to see the brokenness of her husband. Was this the man she had thought he was?

'We must learn from this. And we must go on. There is still a fine garden here to tend. It is the role we have chosen in life. We felt we were chosen, or called to it. Do you remember? The *Manual* says that we are to be strong, to be brave, and not to lose courage. We must go on, husband.'

The man listened to the words, and found himself nodding as she spoke. There was truth in what she said. That was her way–the way of most women, he had learned. She could cut through all that which confused an issue, cut to its core, and see through to the reality that lay underneath.

'Yes, you are right,' he conceded, finally, and slowly. Then he stood, as the embers of the fire flickered into the dark sky.

'Yes,' we must go on,' she said, hugging him tightly.

He nodded.

But in his heart, the truth was very, very hard to accept. And it was the last thing he wanted to face, so he determined in his heart to bury it deeply.

Chapter Nine

*'For all of us have become like one who is
unclean, and all our righteous deeds are like a
filthy garment;
and all of us wither like a leaf,
and our iniquities, like the wind, take us away.'*
(Isaiah 64: 6)

'Would you like to go fishing?' asked a fellow gardener some time later as he walked past the garden entrance.

'I'm sorry. I'm too busy,' said the gardener, looking up from a particularly untidy section of his garden where weeds and a nasty vine had taken root, and were getting a little out of hand.

'That's too bad,' said the passer-by. 'I'm told the waters are full of fish just waiting for some enterprising fisherman to pluck them out.'

Yes, and plants dying from neglect all across the country, the gardener thought to himself. He looked up from his work.

The passer-by was casually, but neatly dressed, and looked a pleasant-enough fellow. The gardener recognised him as a fellow man-of-the-field although he had no real reputation, and his garden was of little consequence. There were many such gardeners popping up these days. Often they were silly young men, men of little real substance, viewing gardening more as a soft working option than as an occupation of great horticultural significance. They were men seeking lucrative financial benefits with as little effort as possible, and were bringing the entire profession into disrepute.

Far too often now, the new breed of gardener was a man who shirked the greater demands of the profession. They were men who had an eye on some eternal reward for their labours, but whose likelihood of achieving it was limited by temporal concerns. Invariably they were men of limited physical size and intellect, and in many cases even less practical skills, who generally compensated for inherent weaknesses with the style of leadership that relied more on dictatorship than consensus. *They* were the leader, *they* had the commission, *they* had all the answers and conviction, and they were reluctant to take advice or listen to anyone of lesser stature. They were also marked as men who lacked any greatness of vision or perspective because they spent more time looking over their shoulder than looking forward.

They were men who grew small gardens, with a small selection of plants, who lacked true courage and conviction, and spent their lifetimes wondering why others always had greater success and recognition than they did. Often they were the type of man who viewed the profession as an opportunity to lay claim to some worth in the community. Too many times they substituted charisma for zeal, and superficiality for character.

Charisma and superficiality were twin evils. Both were masks for a variety of other faults, whether it was simple ineptitude, immorality or even laziness.

This type of man cast a shadow over all gardens.

Gardeners such as these, left true gardeners with heavy hearts, and generated contempt both within and without the plant world.

The gardener offered his hand and the visitor shook it. It was not the grip of a true man-of-the-field, the gardener concluded. There was a weakness in the handshake– a weakness that characterised a man reluctant to work hard, and a softness of skin that suggested it had rarely even been blistered or dirty.

'A man must get away sometimes. He must have a chance to think and plan,' said the passer-by.

'But my garden is more important,' said the gardener, and for the first time realised he had said so with little real conviction. 'There are crops I must harvest before it's too late.'

'I hear you spend all your time in the garden,' replied the passer-by, casting an interested eye over the rows of trees and plants. The almond tree had recently flowered. Delicate blossoms of yellow and white had appeared almost overnight, and presented a rare display. 'And you really do have a splendid garden. But do you need to be in it all the time? Can't the harvest be put off a little while?'

'The *Manual* says the harvest is a large one and should not be put off. Too few of us are actually bringing the harvest in,' replied the gardener.

It was true. There was a lot of activity, a lot of talking and sowing and planting and so on, but it was generally accepted that harvests were thin right across the country. It seemed that more attention was being paid to establishment and maintenance of existing gardens than to actually reaping the harvests. Mostly, they rotted and died in the fields.

'Let them ripen a little longer. The more sun they get, the riper they will be,' countered the visiting gardener. And then, on purpose, he changed the course of the conversation.

'You have gained quite a reputation with this garden,' he said, casting an approving eye across it. 'It is certainly one of the finest gardens I have ever seen. Certainly far better than mine. I really have trouble getting plants to grow. I think it's the soil. Perhaps you can help me.'

The gardener straightened and stretched his back. It took more than good soil he knew, to produce such a fine garden. But the words of the passer-by pleased him, so he held his tongue.

'There are many gardeners, you know, who would like to learn some of the secrets of your success. Someone as successful as you should share with those of us who struggle.'

The words were like honey to the gardener's soul, still grieving inwardly at the loss of his terebinth tree. He looked again at the empty space where it had once stood, now a scar on the landscape not yet healed. He sighed. It hurt him yet, and although he wasn't aware of it, the loss had damaged him more than either he or his wife would admit to themselves.

To some extent, the personal hurt had been largely concealed. In its place, the pride he felt in himself and his accomplishments was becoming more obvious in the comments he made to others about his garden, or in the way he accepted compliments. It was such a difficult thing to come to terms with– pride. The *Manual* spoke much of it, of its dangers, and the gardener believed he genuinely guarded himself well against it. Yet in truth, he *was* proud of what he had achieved, and felt he had a right to be so. Was it such an unnatural emotion?

At the same time, he was also aware of gardeners who were always away from their gardens. These were the ones who cared less about their plants than they did about their reputations, and who constantly justified their absences as being in the best interests of horticulture in general. Why, they would attend conferences with high-sounding titles like *'How to Save Broken Plants'* or *'Reaching the Lost Plants'* or *'Overcoming Root Disease'* or *'Inspiring Plant Growth'* or *'Expanding Your Garden'* and so on. More often or not, they were only junkets.

Such conferences, they would assert, helped them to make other gardens healthy, and after all, they often picked up useful tips themselves which they could also use. Unfortunately, far too often, such knowledge was rarely put into practice, and the conferences were more and more being viewed by the general horticultural societies as being more an excuse by gardeners to push personal barrows in an endeavour to gain some reputation. It was a means by which one garden, and gardener, could achieve some prominence over another.

Still other gardeners only attended such conferences as an excuse to avoid the work back in their gardens for a time, and who proudly displayed their gardening badges without ever really applying the obligations that came with it.

All in all, conferences and seminars were becoming a real growth industry, and more and more garden funds were being channelled into them at the expense of improved planting or harvesting techniques.

It seemed that gardeners everywhere were becoming authors and speakers, or professional conference-attendees, and the crucial role of true gardening was becoming blurred. Energies were being dissipated or becoming deviant, or tangential. And as a consequence, many gardens were becoming untidy, unkempt, or so devoid of plants of any quality that they were rapidly becoming places of community ridicule.

Not that it bothered many of these gardeners. All too often, quality of plant in a garden was secondary to statistics– and like all statistics, was open to abuse or falsification.

In one place where the number of plants was small, the gardener might argue that numbers wasn't the most important criteria– endeavouring to improve plant quality was. But in another, where plants proliferated and the gardener was continually extending his borders, he would argue the case that quantity was the essential rule of thumb, and that quality was of secondary concern.

That's not to say there weren't exceptions to the rule.

From time to time, there were visiting gardeners whose carriage and words marked them as legitimate people worth listening to. They came from gardens where excellence was a by-word, and in their demeanour one could easily discern the true gardening heart and spirit. And in the gardens they visited, this was obvious in the assistance they provided the local gardener, with obvious discernible improvement in the overall garden.

But they were rare.

The truth was, most gardeners felt that they had something of substance to add to the general knowledge of gardening technique, and if they were honest with themselves, longed for opportunities to present their viewpoint to interested audiences.

It came down to a question of ego and self-esteem with many such men. Never being asked to speak at a gardening conference was as emotionally debilitating as the hard work of gardening maintenance was physically. Most aspired to it, yet few had the skills and expertise to actually do so. This, itself, led to envy and jealousy and ultimately spoiled many a man.

For some time, the gardener had begun to wonder if perhaps there wasn't a balance he could strike in such matters, for up till now he had kept himself out of such goings-on. He understood the necessity for a constant presence in the garden both in working it and in protecting it, but with each passing day, the injuries sustained in its maintenance were taking its toll on him.

Weariness was eating at his spirit. And sometimes he found it difficult to recall the fervour and exhilaration with which he had first proclaimed his decision to garden in the first place.

At the same time, he now spent very little time on personal inner reflection or study. And while his wife had upheld him as best she could, sustaining him with all the strength and determination she could muster, it could not compensate for his own failure to do so.

So as the passer-by stood at the gate, it was a man weakened both spiritually and physically who met his gaze. And such a man was at the mercy of those who would pull his garden down.

'We could speak of gardening things,' said the passer-by, pressing his advantage, arresting the gardener's thoughts. 'Such men as us need to spend time together, supporting each other, and talking of things to do with gardening. There is much we could share, and we could relax at the same time.'

'Yes,' said the gardener finally, letting the weed in his hand fall back to the soil. 'Perhaps I could spend a little time away. There should be no harm in it.'

CHAPTER TEN

*'Pride goes before destruction, and a haughty
spirit before stumbling.'*
(Proverbs 16:18)

And so it was that a significant change came over the gardener.

Over time, he began to look at his garden in a new light.

Before, it was all he had lived for. It was the very reason and essence of his being. It was something he had put together with his own hands and the strength of his arms. He had given birth to it, shaped it, and now it stood firmly established in the community as a singular bastion of gardening principles perfectly executed.

But suddenly, ever since that first fishing trip, and with new insights that came from seminars and conferences he had also started to attend, he came to appreciate the garden from a different perspective.

As Autumn days closed over the garden once again, he began to realise that it wasn't himself that had breathed life into the garden after all. And now that it was truly established, a greater Power than he exercised control over it, and his role now only complimented or detracted from it.

Responsibility for the garden began to shift from his shoulders, and he saw no error in his logic. As he began to see it, he had largely done his part and since a greater Power than he was responsible for the garden, then surely that greater Power could exercise a certain responsibility for its maintenance as well.

Unfortunately, he was unaware that there was another power loose within the garden, and within himself, and that it was the gardener himself who had inadvertently let it in.

It was a spirit of destruction, manifested in blight and disease and a sea of weeds.

* * *

What the gardener had failed to notice, and what casual observers (not to mention other gardeners) had also failed to notice, was that beneath the superficial beauty of the garden, subtle changes had begun to take place.

Actually, they had first begun a long time earlier during that period in which the great terebinth tree had started to die.

While the battle to save it had taken place, it was as if the whole garden had held its collective breath; and when it had finally died, it seemed as if something of the garden and the gardener's vitality had been sapped along with it.

It happened slowly, and the changes were manifest in various forms.

'Weeds!' cried his wife one day, working among the seedlings.

'Weeds?' echoed the gardener, resting in a hammock strung between two of his larger trees. It was one of his favourite spots in the garden–supported by strong trees, shaded, a place to rest and be restored.

'Yes weeds!' she said, with just a trace of sarcasm. 'You remember what they look like? They're everywhere!'

Well of course they are, he thought. What garden doesn't have weeds of some sort? It seemed to him that he had been fighting a never-ending battle with them from day one.

'I try my best,' he said wearily. 'But they're hard to keep under control.'

Especially laying in a hammock, his wife thought, but kept the thought to herself. She had sensed the change in her husband, his troubled spirit, his wearied look, and found herself at a loss as to how to help him through it.

Neither did she want to contribute to his distress, for she suspected that his condition was spiritual as well as physical. Peculiarly, he had recently taken to eating only vegetables, and she remembered reading that such a thing was a sure sign of a man in a weakened state.

'Yes, you do,' she agreed. 'But we aren't being as effective as we used to be. They are sucking all the nutrients from the soil. And some are actually beginning to strangle some of our smaller plants. And husband,' she said, with a hint of annoyance in her voice, 'they look untidy. It reflects badly on us.'

He knew she was right. But his drive was gone. Without even realising it, he had lost that essential strength and conviction that burned in the best gardeners. An overpowering tiredness had beset him.

'And insects,' she continued. 'They're attacking a lot of our plants. And look at the state of some of these leaves,' she added, almost shoving them into his face. 'They're covered in blight and fungus.'

She softened momentarily, realising there was anger and condemnation in her voice.

'Husband,' she almost pleaded, 'our garden is deteriorating. There are plants suffering. There is something dreadfully wrong. It is our fault.'

But, she meant it was *his* fault.

The gardener's mind though was racing ahead of his wife's.

'Perhaps we could hire an assistant,' he said, almost as an idle thought. It was something he had thought about a lot lately. Now he was testing the waters. He knew his wife had often proved to be a fine sounding board, and he valued her intuition.

He did not expect her response to be so abrupt.

'An assistant?' she almost yelled at him. 'No real gardener hires an assistant! A man who would work a garden only for the wages he could earn does not belong in a garden. Assistants ruin a garden,' she continued, red-faced with anger. 'They run them down, or undermine the true gardener. They would take what they had no part in building up. With assistant gardeners, no plant is safe because there is no heartfelt concern behind their work.'

She looked at her husband. Coldness clouded her eyes. Then she continued.

'An assistant is an assistant because he lacks the courage and spiritual commitment to strike out on his own. It's the easy route to prominence in our area of work. But you *know* this, husband. You have seen for yourself assistant gardeners who come into a garden, say all the right words, and win over the gardener with all sorts of promises. But in their hearts there is something else. They are motivated by ambition, usually disguised, or greed for position or power, and spend their days working against the true gardener, and against the true interests of gardening. Oh you'll see them in the garden all right, re-shaping here, re-defining boundaries there, busying themselves among the plants. But husband, it's all show. Their true motives are hidden.'

'That's not entirely true,' he replied frostily. 'Many a garden has room for an assistant and not all assistant gardeners are deviate. Circumstances may simply preclude them having a garden of their own most of the time. To generalise like you have done, is to perpetrate an unfairness. What about women who don't have a partner, yet have the same heartfelt desire to build a garden?'

'If they have such a heart,' said the wife, 'then the Master Gardener will bring it about. I'm not saying it's not impossible. Women are often purer of heart and motive, but it is their very femininity, the very nature of womanhood, their fragility if you like, that poses particular problems in respect of the work concerned. That's not to say they are not as capable as most men of doing the job, in fact, in many instances we both are aware of, they are more capable than some, and mostly have a compassion and sensitivity men can only hope to ever have. But the particular demands of some aspects of gardening need the strength of a man's arm, not a woman's. No,' she added, 'it's not a woman I'm afraid of. It's the weakling man who lacks the initiative to follow his own dream, to set out on his own, and latches on to one such as you to fulfil his own desires.'

She paused, her anger largely spent. Then she made the final point.

'There will not be an assistant in *this* garden,' she stated in a manner that left no room for argument, or further discussion. 'We already have more than enough problems.'

'Would you rather the garden go into decline? Can't you see that I'm weary?'

'I would rather that you trust in Him who put us here,' she said softly. 'It is His garden after all. Not ours. He will do what is necessary.'

He did not argue further, but tossed the matter around a little more in his mind. It was true that assistants had little credibility in the profession, despite the fact that many were as proficient, if not even more effective than the gardeners themselves. Yes, he thought, an assistant could help carry some of the burden. While I'm helping others, he would be helping me. But a look at his wife's face told him to let the matter rest for the moment.

There was no gain in a confrontation with her at this time. It was what he liked most about her. He respected her forthrightness, and her intuitive sense about the loftier aspects of their work. He was aware that while his communion with the Master Gardener had become vague and unsubstantial, hers had never wavered.

He often felt guilty about it, but she had seemed to become stronger as he had declined in spirit, and that pleased him. There was a strength about her that carried them both.

'You used to dig the weeds out completely, once,' she continued, knowing there would be no further talk of *assistants* for a while. In her eyes there were matters to be dealt with of more significance than pipe-dreams. 'But now you only pull out the obvious growth, and the roots stay in the ground. As soon as you walk away they almost grow straight back again!'

Unaware of it, she cried now as she spoke. 'And there was a time when no insect or disease would affect our garden. You were a different man then,' she added, sadly, falling to her knees. Then she gave away to a sudden, muffled sobbing.

The gardener was moved to go to her and console her, but her tirade had caught him by surprise. He felt his heart harden a little toward her.

In truth, he could care less about her criticisms. And the crying bothered him little. At the recent conference on *'Negativity in the Garden'* which he had attended with some fellow, local gardeners he had become firm friends with, the theme had been about the danger of negative words and actions in the garden. *'Negativity breeds negativity!'* had been the conference catch-phrase, and the gardeners who attended had taken it to heart.

There was some considerable truth in the matter, of course. The correlation between positive thought and productivity was a well-documented fact of much gardening literature which lined the shelves of many a gardener's library. In essence, gardeners who had positive thoughts about the growth of their gardens or the current state of the plants already in them, would reap positive results of a material kind.

But there was a fundamental weakness in such a narrow-minded approach. Many of the gardeners had taken it to mean that *all* negative comments were counter-productive, whether it was about their gardens, their plants, their methods, or themselves! Therefore they never listened to any negative criticism, regardless of whether or not it was constructive or not, and rather than accept it, or even contemplate it, they chose to ignore it and lived a lie.

The gardener swung in his hammock and enjoyed the intellectual arguments he could have with himself now that he was associating with such stimulating company.

The conferences had enlightened him, and had increased his knowledge of gardening aspects many-fold. Wonderful speakers had made light of many of the more complex sections of the *Manual* and this too pleased him. He had found it much too difficult to bother with to any great extent now, and anyway his free time had always been limited. And if someone else could explain the deeper meanings of the more obscure sections and he was able to use it to promote the cause of gardening, what could be wrong with that?

As well, he had also begun to speak at these conferences, although a little reluctant at first. But a gardener who had such obvious talents really needed to share his secrets with fellow gardeners who perhaps had not been as endowed with such talents as he. So he had accepted a number of such speaking engagements, and found that he was very well received. So much so, in fact, that he was rapidly becoming something of a celebrity, and the mantle rested easily on his shoulders.

It was ironic, he thought, that one who had spent so little time actually studying the *Manual* (due to the time he spent in the garden) was now considered an expert on all gardening matters. More and more often he was called away to speak here and there, and his status within the ranks of gardeners rose dramatically.

'I've been thinking,' he said one day to his wife, breaking an awkward silence that had hung between the two, 'that perhaps I was meant to do greater things than run a garden. People have told me that the world

needs many more gardens like mine, and that maybe
I'm just the person to start a great move of horticulture
across the country. They say my garden is among the
finest of its type anywhere in the world, and obviously
I've done something right!'

His wife dried her tears and got to her feet. She
had been listening to similar comments from him for
some time now, ever since he had begun to run with
'idlers' as she called them. It concerned her greatly.
She was unsure of how to react. After all, he *was* the
gardener, and he had done the great bulk of the work
himself. And he had been enormously successful, she
had to admit. For her part, she accepted her station as
his help-mate, and who was she to question his vision?

'It must be more than men who would need to
confirm such an idea,' she said. 'And only you know if
you have been given greater plans for our lives.'

Well, it *had* been confirmed, he realised. His
garden had been exceptionally blessed, and was much
admired in the community, and by his peers. His
reputation was such that there were calls for him to
speak at Gardening rallies and Conferences all across
the country, not to mention the local community where
struggling gardeners eagerly sought out his advice.

He had sown, and he was reaping a great
reward for his diligence. In each success, there was
confirmation that greater exploits were expected
of him.

And so he began to dwell on the thought– his
'visionary role' as he called it. And what a vision it

was! To plant gardens all across the country, and then raise up other gardeners to work them.

It was a vision to be dwelt on, as he lay on his hammock and watched the chilly winds sweep across a grey, bleak sky.

'We'll see what the future holds,' he said. 'It's going to be a cold Autumn,' he announced grandly, and casting a cursory glance over the garden, closed his eyes. The conversation was over.

And as he slept, insidious forces were changing the face of his garden forever, and he, completely oblivious to them, slept on.

CHAPTER ELEVEN

'For where envying and strife is,
there is confusion and every evil work'
(James 3: 16)

The garden deteriorated at a remarkable rate.

While to some extent, the changes had begun with the gardener's preoccupation with saving the terebinth tree and the limited amount of time he had spent in his garden as the tree died, it was also much to do with his pursuit of grandeur.

It was something his wife had tried her best to counteract, but she had neither the strength, nor depth of gardening insight to allow her to compensate for his brooding, or his absence.

Her failure to do so, irritated her. She had failed him. And in the failure, as she perceived it, man had won another battle.

It was a point upon which she often reflected. It appeared that men seemed to have an innate capacity to rise to the major gardening positions in most gardening societies. Women, to a great extent, didn't. Where they *had*, it seemed the situation was only temporary, or short-lived. Some major difficulty would arise, or the garden would quickly show signs of disrepair, and critics would jump to the conclusion that a woman simply didn't seem to have the necessary capabilities to do the job adequately.

She never really understood why. It seemed to her that women were just as capable as any man. They were widely acclaimed for their sensitivities to the finer points of gardening, and more often than not appeared to be more in tune with the very forces that operated within gardens than men did. And her study of the *Manual* suggested that women were regarded highly, and even more so perhaps than men were by the Master Gardener Himself.

Certainly there was widespread appreciation outside the garden, that female gardeners were often just as capable, as sensitive, and as intuitive than any male gardener. They seemed to have greater depth of character, less moral and ethical weakness, and were more finely tuned to the demands of the profession as instructed by the *Manual*.

Yet the opportunities for full-time managerial positions were few and far between, and when one did eventuate in a particular garden, opposition could be quite brutal-even from other women. Some, (mostly men) would run to their *Manual*, and locate obscure references that appeared to limit the role of women in gardens. That those references were written for the earliest gardeners and for far less sophisticated gardens than now existed, was an irrelevancy that men glossed over. It appeared that men, usually men lacking in ability and self-esteem themselves, would use the references at every opportunity to limit women's involvement in gardens everywhere.

At the same time, she was aware that in some gardens where the gardener was known to be something of a weakling, and where the wife had attempted to fill the void, a certain devastation had been wrought. It had been as if even the plants themselves resented the female touch. Some of these women simply lacked the strength. Others, the heart. Others simply had an inflated opinion of their own abilities, an opinion not shared by others, nor verified, nor divinely-inspired. Such a temperament proved to be more destructive.

The gardener's wife understood this. It was simply the way it was. All the carping, and rhetoric and debate in the world wasn't about to change the great majority of men's minds about women in control of gardens, so she accepted it.

She had long ago reconciled herself to only being a helper to her husband, and having little managerial input.

So now, despite the parlous state of the garden, there was precious little she could do but sit back and watch, and put her faith in the Master, believing that whatever was meant to be, would eventuate in due course.

As for the changes taking place in the garden, she was completely powerless. She could only sit back and wait for the inevitable, for she sensed what was about to happen. A reckoning was due. But perception of, and the ability to alter a situation, were two different things.

What was true, was that the deterioration of the garden reflected the duality of the gardener's current existence– something neither the gardener nor his wife were aware of. As he faltered as a man and as a gardener, so too did the garden fall away. The changes were not necessarily overt, or immediately obvious. It was a simple process of deterioration where the garden mirrored the man.

And most dangerously of all, the man himself failed to notice it. Or at least, he failed to acknowledge it publicly to anyone but himself.

On the one hand, he felt charged with a new appreciation of his worth and his importance as a gardener of great renown. Now, no longer was it only his garden that was the centre of public acclaim, but also the man himself. When he moved around the community, no longer did he dress in the humble clothes of the gardener, but more and more in the suits and coats of an aspiring Grand Horticulturist, the highest of earthly ranks in his field. And being a Grand Horticulturist was a great honour for any gardener to aspire to, the pinnacle of the profession.

But on the other hand, he was secretly plagued by doubt which infected his heart and soul. It was something he was very careful to conceal. The doubts were overwhelming. Doubts about the very nature of gardening, doubts about the actual gardening processes, doubts about gardening as a noble profession or as a way of life, doubts about his motives, his capabilities, his very existence.

The spirit of doubt had entered the man after the death of the terebinth, and had profoundly affected him as time wore on. While he never showed it publicly, the doubts had permeated his gardening spirit, sucking him into an emotional whirlpool– a psychological crisis that tore at him daily.

It sapped the strength of his arm, and pricked at his conscience. And where before, he had pursued his occupation with an unadulterated idealism and enthusiasm, now he even questioned that very calling.

When death visited the garden, as it had, all sorts of questions were asked of gardeners. Were they failures themselves, as individuals or as leaders? Was there a weakness in the manner they administered their gardens? Was there a failure to adhere to correct technique?

And so on. Every critic had an opinion.

And He often thought of that strange man who had set him upon this road so many years ago, and wondered why he hadn't been more forthright in demanding more information from him then.

Now it was too late. The certainty of those early years was long gone, and the irony was that now he was a powerful force in something about which very real doubts now plagued him.

So, caught in the gulf of uncertainty, torn between ambition and debilitating self-doubt, the gardener walked through his garden more and more like a man who had lost his sense of direction in life. And his eyesight.

Chapter Twelve

*'People who want to get rich fall
into temptation and a snare and many
foolish and harmful desires that plunge men
into ruin and destruction.'*

(1 Tim 6: 9)

The changes that had taken place within the garden were obvious to any who looked closely, but the gardener's eyes were closed to them. His natural eyes might have seen them, but not the discerning inner eye that could have convicted his soul of the state of its disrepair.

In the centre of his garden, the showpiece area where the gardener had lavished so much of his time and love in those early days, the sorriest sights were most evident.

The tallest trees, planted for shade and stability and to provide the focal point for garden enthusiasts, were now but shadows of their previous glories. It was as if their wholeness had been spent in competition with each other. They had grown tall, certainly, and were still the most conspicuous plants in the garden, but their vitality seemed to have been lost in the struggle for height, rather than substance. Their canopies, meant to be full and thick with foliage, were sparse and straggly. No longer did they complement each other as they had when first the garden had been planted out. Instead, as they had striven to reach above the other for the fullest sun and the first of the rains, or had clawed to gain the gardener's special attentions, their effectiveness in the overall plan of the central garden area was lost.

Highest, was a straight but limbless tree. It had reached highest, and although successful in that aim, lacked the luxuriant growth that comes with full maturity. It was as if its energies had been expended in the desire for height, and so it stood, tall and narrow and of little substance or worth.

In a gully, a skeleton of a tree stood starkly against the green backdrop. The first of all the trees in this area to die, it seemed as if it had suddenly lost some vital component during its growth. Up to a point it had been fine, but whereas others had gone on to higher levels, it had not. Unable to maintain the same growth rate, or perhaps due to some innate deficiency or weakness, or perhaps even a certain neglect by the gardener at a critical time in its growth, it had simply stopped growing, and died where it stood. Soon it would fall and join those other trees wasting away on the ground.

Even the greatest of oaks had suffered. Although still a stunning specimen of tree, close to its base a large protuberance of sap had formed like a boil on its trunk. Rather than being pumped through the tree to the highest points where the sap could have exploded in its richness through the boughs and leaves, it hadn't. Instead, it had formed an odd, unsightly mass, closer to the ground. While it did not appear to affect the overall appearance of the tree, neither did it enhance it. In truth, its full potential was never going to be realised.

The situation was no better with the lesser trees and shrubs. Those that had been planted to create an atmosphere of colour and harmony, essential to every garden, were faring poorly. Denied full access to the life-blood of the seasons, struggling for root space with the trees that towered above them, they had begun to spread their growth outwards. Now, unpruned and decidedly untidy, their branches clashed one against the other, leaving them all scarred and broken.

Any blooms that managed to appear here were of poor quality and almost lifeless in colour.

In the orchards where good fruit had grown on apparently healthy trees, they now hung spoiled. On the trees, they had looked fine, but the gardener's failure to adequately inspect and spray them had left them rotten and filled with maggots. Other trees in this area produced no fruit at all, their leaves and branches covered in scales, or mottled with blight from a poisonous root, or from wormwood. Here, where pruning should have been completed much earlier, the trees were a tangled mess of untidy branches and the fruit of very poor quality, soured and fly-blown.

Even in the seed-beds, the new plants that had been specially sown by the gardener himself, drooped from lack of attention. They, too, had long since failed to receive water or fertiliser of any quality or quantity, and some had already fallen away. Others seemed to gasp for sustenance, struggling within themselves to stay alive, their leaves withered and almost lifeless.

Not surprisingly, even the rockery was in chaos. Plants from this area were now out of control, had broken from their beds and were sprouting across the garden proper. Plants of thorn and spike now were growing alongside plants of infinitely greater character, and according to their natural abrasiveness, cut deeply into the bark of the finer plants, wounding them badly. Ivy had spread quickly, and now wound itself around trees everywhere, slowly strangling the life-blood from them.

So it was in all other areas of the garden.

Lifelessness pervaded almost every plant of any consequence. Those lesser plants, the plants that are grown in large numbers and which, in quantity give a garden its relative claim to 'health' stood listless and yellowing. Many could survive in such a state for some time, and for many it was even the pinnacle of growth. But they were not the plants they should have been, or could have been. It was as if their access to the sun had been denied by days of long, cloudy skies which yielded no rain. And so now, they stood dormant and fruitless, their vitality sapped.

But there were two exceptions.

The first was the fig tree. It stood in a meadow, framed by the edges of a looming escarpment, and guarding a valley that fell away to the northern areas of the garden. It was the finest expression of plant life in the garden. Its base was short, but thick and solid. Huge roots plunged into the earth on all sides. From such a base, solid and immovable, a myriad of branches struck out in every direction, each covered in a glistening foliage and rich fruit. In full bloom, it spoke of an assuredness, a richness of purpose, an even mix of blessings, and when a gentle wind moved across it, it would lift its leaves to the heavens to soak in every measure of life.

Around it, clinging vines had sought to strangle it, or hold it back. But in this instance, they had had no effect whatsoever, other than to detract a little from its beauty.

The flower beds, too, were an exception. Here, change had taken place as well, but the changes had been more subtle, less obtrusive.

For here, among the delicate blooms and sweet fragrances, the gardener had found a place where he could find peace in body and soul. More and more he had felt compelled to be among them rather than in other areas of the garden.

Here, there had been less likelihood of his being hurt amongst the soft blooms and soil than in some of the harsher areas where the stronger, wilder plants had been set in place. More than any other of his plants, they had seemed to respond warmly to his attentions, and so he had given them more.

And it was true that his very presence seemed to bring out a depth of richness of colour in their blooms, and a brightness and vitality in their leaves that might not normally have been there.

Nevertheless, despite his presence, despite the time he devoted to them, the corruption that was in the plant world at large, and which had now pervaded the whole garden, was also manifested in the flower beds, though the gardener was oblivious to it there as well.

He noted only that a particular rose has soared in height, and produced blooms of great complexity, rich in fragrance and subtlety of colour. As he has said it would, its very positioning in the bed had enhanced the whole garden, drawing out the best of colour and fragrance of every other flower.

Even the narcissi, usually resplendent and among the most attractive of flowers, paled into insignificance beside it.

The gardener had often stood beside the rose, drinking in its great beauty, and all the time he failed to see how the lesser roses had reacted. Neither as dominant or as attractive, their blooms inferior in every respect, unable to match the rose in any regard, they had taken to encroaching upon its root space, sapping its very grasp on life. They had even locked thorn-laden branches with it, as if they would either use it as leverage to drag themselves up to a similar height, or tear it down to their level.

It was where his wife joined him on one occasion as he walked among them, stroking each one gently, lost in thought.

'You spend much time here, my husband,' she said coldly. 'And the time is wasted.'

He stared at her, almost right through her. 'Why is it wasted?' he asked, though he no longer really cared about what she might say.

'It is wasted because they are simply not as productive as most other plants,' she said, her heart heavy with trepidation at what she was about to say.

The gardener did not want to respond, despite the apparent contradiction in her earlier philosophy. He knew she would push him into doing so eventually anyway, so he said,

'That's not the case at all. The flowers in our garden are quite significant. I've rarely seen better specimens in all my travels.'

'Yes, we've done a great job in that regard,' his wife replied. 'But flowers are only part of our garden, not the essence of it. They are certainly fine, and their contribution to the aesthetics of the garden can't be denied. And yes, they are a special species....very special,' and now her heart winced as she spoke, 'but flowers catch only fleeting glances from the outside world. They *look* good, and when harvested can be of great worth. But because of their relative size and the quantity of them, and the effort that is expended on them, they are not as valuable as our major resources. They are, to some extent, almost expendable resources. In truth, it is the tallest trees, the loftiest shrubs, the evergreen bushes that really dictate the relative strength and success of a garden. It is in their size, their potency, their inherent strength that determines the viability of our venture. It is them that makes our garden better than others. It is there that the worth of our garden is measured, not in flowers. Not even with our flowers, and not even with our roses.'

The gardener stood quite still, shocked at the unexpected outburst. He had felt that a woman, more than any other, would understand the implicit importance of flowers in the overall make-up of a garden.

'But our garden was to be a garden where all plants of all description could grow to their full potential,' he replied wearily, 'and to do so as healthily as they can. It was never to be a garden where one plant was considered more important, more prominent, than another, except in relation to their positioning.'

'Yet, despite all your experience, despite all these long, hard years, you have missed an essential truth of gardening,' she answered back. 'And that is, that it is the very nature of plants that one will grow bigger and bolder and more prominently than another; that the timber of some will prove more valuable than that of another; that even among flowers, some will be more delicate, more aromatic in perfume than another. You know these things. That's why you took such great care with your planning all that time ago. And you must remember, right back then that flowers were very much an afterthought in your overall plan for this garden, almost an irrelevance. Almost like it was in Eden.'

The gardener pondered her words. But his oratory and intellect were much superior to hers these days, and his experience on both a practical and theoretical level much more developed.

But my dear wife,' he said, 'you see for yourself that some of our blooms are among our most valuable assets, greatly desired by other gardeners, and we are always at risk of losing them to unscrupulous gardeners. Look at our home-grown orchids for example. Some of them are so perfectly developed, so beautiful, so rich in colour and rare in number that they are worth more than any tree. What you aren't aware of is that in many gardens, flowers are the very backbone of the enterprise. Why I've even seen gardens where not only are flowers the chief produce, the gardens are actually managed by female gardeners.'

She looked at him oddly. Such strange talk, she thought. She had never known him to utter such strange thoughts, such different arguments to those he once clung to.

'And they are the first gardens to be washed away in a storm,' she answered back

It had been a curious exchange, she thought. Here was a man, who, long ago, had planned in intricate detail every aspect of the garden. He had confirmed such a plan in accordance with the *Manual* and personal spiritual communion. Now though, when their garden had reached a certain level of maturity, he was still debating the relative merits of individual plants and species, and seemed to have developed a curious fascination for flowers.

With each passing day, she had found him more distant, and more and more less in control of the garden and himself.

'Even here, where you seem to find a great need to be, lately,' she said, spreading her arms over the flower beds, 'the work has not been done as it should be. Indeed, our entire garden is suffering, one way or another.'

She held his arm by the elbow, and led him to a plain-looking flower tucked away in a dark corner of one of the beds.

'Look under your feet,' she continued. 'For some time I watched a bloom develop on that plant, more beautiful than any I have ever seen. As beautiful as any rose,' she added dryly, glancing across at the roses he admired so much. 'But because of its plainness, its unattractive outward appearance, you walked by it many times without even glancing at it. Today, it is gone, destroyed by the first blast of the winter wind, and lies crushed under your heel.'

'Then you should have picked it yourself, wife,' he answered, a rising anger in his voice, and realising the pettiness of the conversation. He had much to do and prepare for, and his time with the flowers was one of relaxation and an opportunity to think more clearly about his plans. He held such time to be beneficial to his own well-being. To have it taken from him annoyed him considerably.

'If you were the gardener you once were,' she said, 'you would have seen that bloom long ago, nurtured it, and plucked it long before it fell away. It is a fault I have seen in you much of late. I have seen so many beautiful blooms in these beds, and they were blooms you greatly admired. But what you did not see was that it was *those* very blooms that wilted first in the noon day sun, or lost their petals in the first draughts of autumn. There was no substance in them. But you prized them just because they were bigger, or brighter, or more beautiful than another, whereas in truth, they were but gaudy and superficial– the least in your garden. How could you have got things so wrong?'

She almost spat the words at him now, such was the rising anger in her.

And there she left him. Without another word, she turned and left him alone with his thoughts.

The gardener watched her go. Her rebuke didn't bother him all that much. There were things he simply want to hear about himself, or his garden.

Some truths he had already seen for himself. After all, he wasn't a stupid man. And yet, paradoxically, even those truths fuelled his flagging self-esteem. They intrigued him. Could a gardener be so capable as to build a garden of such magnificence, and earn such widespread acclaim for it, yet still be so ignorant?

He thought not.

The fact was, his wife had only discerned half the truth. Some, the gardener had already realised about himself well before his wife had. And ironically, it had been among his most fancied roses that he had first confronted his personal failures.

One day, as he had tended his plants, he had dwelt far longer among the roses than he had intended. Idly tending them, he found it to be his favourite part of the garden these days, and far less hard work than other sections.

It was then that he first noticed that not all his roses, which he fancied above all other plants, offered up a perfume. They looked beautiful, elegant even, and appeared to be full of fragrance, but for many of them it was all illusion.

In fact, (and his wife had already hinted at this, being more familiar with the species than any male gardener) he observed that the most beautiful of roses, those with the most delicate hues of colour and delicate petals, those with the most wondrous of perfume, came not from the most prominently planted roses, but the lowliest and plainest of the flower species.

And he came to realise as a truism that some flowers never bloomed at all. In all gardens he had learned, there were plants such as these– plants that grew to a particular height and shape and stayed there, irregardless of any further measures to improve, despite there being ample evidence in the *Manual* that growth was something every plant could expect until it was time to die. Others responded for a while, but unless they were tended religiously, soon drooped and wilted.

The gardener saw in such plants a reflection of personal failure, and could easily have accepted full blame and responsibility for it, but rational thought often won out.

After all, peculiarities of plant life– like retarded growth and the failure to bloom– were not confined just to *his* garden. All gardens everywhere endured such problems, though most managed to hide the disappointments or moved them to less prominent areas to camouflage the extent of the problem.

So the gardener adopted a simple premise for such failures– if they were manifest in all gardens, why should his be any different? Why should he flagellate himself over a few failures when gardeners who had never reached his level of competence rarely held themselves accountable– writing such aberrations off as a normal consequence of gardening? Why should his garden be any different to any other in this regard? Did anyone have the right to condone him for minor failings when the overall impression of his garden, taken by others, was that it was a far healthier enterprise than many of the smaller gardens cropping up all over the place?

He thought not.

*　　*　　*

Actually, the gardener's preoccupation with the flowers greatly troubled his wife.

As a woman, she was much more alert to the dangers that lay in flower beds than many male gardeners were aware of, simply because they were men, after all. She knew that some of the world's most beautiful flowers also contained the most deadly poisons. She knew in her heart that all gardeners' wives held the safety of their husbands in their own hands. When a wife was lax in her obligations, the gardener would fall.

It was a worldwide phenomena.

'The *Manual* warns us about the dangers of some plants,' she reminded him one day, in a somewhat admonishing tone. 'Their thorns can cause great sickness, even unto death.'

She had repeated the warning often, more so in later days, because she sensed him drifting away from her, and from the great commission they had embarked upon.

Not that he needed to be warned. All gardeners were well aware of the inherent dangers of the trade, *the three F's* as they were called– Finance! Fame! And Flowers! They were written on every gardener's soul as indelible signposts on the road to eventual destruction.

Yet every day, gardeners fell by the wayside because they ignored the warnings.

Unfortunately, either because he had long since failed to maintain a personal obligation to adhere to the *Manual's* instructions for gardening care, or because he had wandered far from the guidance of the Master Gardener, the gardener's senses had long since dulled. The warnings of his wife fell on deaf ears.

So it was one evening, while the harvest fields waved in a golden afternoon sun, as fruit fell rotting to the ground, and as plants that once had stood tall began to wilt from lack of care, the gardener fell victim to the poison of a singularly poisonous flower.

It was a flower of no great show, neither pretentious in display nor form, but a flower of such magnetism that it attracted the gardener to it, and of late, down in the relative quiet of the flower bed, he had given himself over to its care, above all other plants in the garden.

Then, on one otherwise innocuous afternoon, in a careless, unguarded moment, it struck him a fatal blow as he bent to caress it. He felt at once its poison pour into his body where the thorn had pricked his skin, and knew at once the wound was fatal.

The plant had been mentioned much in the *Manual*, its excesses of colour clearly described, and the effects of its poison made known to every man. Strangely, the poison was addictive, drawing the victim time and time again to the very flower that had struck him down. And with each new strike, the effects of the poison was magnified and cumulative, and any prospect of a cure irrevocably dashed.

It was like a drug in the very marrow of his bones, debilitating his body and crippling his mind, and cutting him off from the one source that could have cured him– the very Master he had set out to serve.

He also knew that not only had he damned himself, but his wife and garden, as well. He knew that he had joined those ranks of gardeners whose gardens and lives had been destroyed by the vilest of plants– and destroyed because of their lusts for that which lay beyond the true call of gardening.

He walked from the garden that day a defeated man.

Wounded, bleeding and dying, he looked over the expanse of his garden, and suddenly saw what he had done in a brilliant clarity. The poison that was killing his body also cleared his mind, and opened his eyes to all that he had done.

And left undone.

And as he watched, a storm appeared on the horizon. Rolling masses of thick cloud, grey, now grey-green, now black and deadly, loomed high in the heavens and bore down upon the garden.

The gardener could only watch its approach with abject despair and the awareness that he alone had brought this upon them both.

CHAPTER THIRTEEN

'How often is the lamp of the wicked put out.
Or does their calamity fall on them?
Does God apportion destruction in His anger?
Are they as straw before the wind,
And like chaff which the storm carries away?'

(Job 21: 17-18)

The storm swept in from the south, odd in itself, and blocked out the sun of day, leaving only a threatening, red sky to frame the ugly swirling mountain of terror bearing down upon the garden.

The gardener hurried home as the sky turned black. His wife was waiting for him. She looked him in the eye, and knew instinctively that he was lost.

'Poisoned?' she asked, though she had no need to ask.

'Yes,' he said meekly, and with that single word, felt the wound to her heart as well as his own.

'Then you are not a man,' she said coldly, turning from him. 'Nor are you a gardener. You are but a shadow of both. You have brought this upon us. And you alone are to blame.'

He nodded, condemned.

'We must hide,' he said madly, his wild eyes searching for a hiding place.

'No,' she said. 'You will face the consequences like a man yet. There is nowhere to hide. We shall face it together.'

And the woman held out her hand to the husband.

He took her hand, wiped tears from his eyes.

'We will shelter as best we can,' he said, avoiding her eyes.

Together, yet apart, they walked out into the garden, and into the very teeth of the storm.

*　　*　　*

Darkness descended upon the garden as if a thick, black shroud had been suddenly draped over it. Over and around the garden, flashes of lightning and peals of thunder exploded simultaneously, fanning the storm onwards.

Suddenly it seemed to rear upwards like a gigantic anvil, then struck the garden with such savagery it was as if a wrath and grief had been hurled from on high by a Power far greater than human comprehension.

The gardener had experienced many storms as the seasons had come and gone, but none that rivalled that which now hammered the garden. Storms had usually come at the end of day and left a trail of minor damage. They were a feature of gardens everywhere, and all gardeners learned to prepare for them as best they could, and tried to limit the damage.

In most storms, damage to gardens was usually minimal, amounting to some broken branches here and there, or a minor plant or two blown away. On rare occasions a tree might have fallen, but only if its position in the garden had been a matter of poor judgement on the gardener's part, or shallow roots by the tree itself. It was the one thing a gardener couldn't really tell– just how deeply-rooted any tree really was. What went on under the surface was anyone's guess.

Once, a particularly savage downpour had threatened to flood the low-lying sections of his garden along with a host of new plants he had raised up, but the gardener's careful placement of rock in the early days, along with the intelligent planting of weeping willows at the water's edge, had prevented major damage. On that occasion, quality plants that might otherwise have been lost in the swirl of mud and water had been saved, and restored.

But not on this occasion. The reckoning had indeed come.

The couple cowered beneath the full fury of the storm. Vainly they sought shelter beneath the larger trees– the myrtles and firs and great she-oaks, but there was no real refuge anywhere. It was what was meant to be. Whatever cover there was, was soon torn away as wind and sleet tore through thick canopies and stripped the trees bare, sending a cascade of leaves and branches down around the pair.

Then the rain turned to hail, as if the very floodgates of heaven were opened, and the sound of its roar was like a cry of great anguish reverberating across the heavens and crashing onto the ground, tearing and ripping its way into the earth. It cut and scourged the bodies of both the man and the woman, for neither the one nor the other seemed to be less at fault. Their bodies were slashed and beaten until their blood ran freely into the sodden earth, and seeped into the garden.

In horror they watched as a single bolt of lightning struck the earth and rolled into a ball of pure blue, electric energy, then lurch against one of the huge oak trees. The tree, which had survived many great storms as it grew, shivered and shuddered and groaned, then fell with an almighty crash upon an entire bed of flowering, dwarf shrubs. A wave of mud and broken branches surged away from the impact.

Impenetrable sheets of rain ripped across the garden tearing foliage to shreds, uprooting seemingly solid plants of all sizes.

They watched in awe and fascination that belied their wretched state as floodwaters, gently rising by the minute, lifted the fallen oak like a matchstick, and carried it towards the flower beds and the rock, retaining wall. With an ear-splitting din of scraping and bursting and splintering of all that lay before it, the wave of trees and debris and mud smashed its way across the landscape. In an instant, and with a roar that echoed above the noise of the storm, it smote the wall and destroyed it. A torrent of irreplaceable trees and topsoil were washed away forever, along with the dreams of the gardeners.

The couple clung to each other as the tempest raged around them, unable to close their eyes to the spectacle. It was almost as if it was meant to be burned into their souls forever.

The flower gardens all but vanished in a matter of moments, taking both the grand and the lesser plants at the same time. The rose that poisoned the gardener was torn out by its roots and blown completely from the earth. The other roses held on tenaciously for a time, but despite the depth and strength of their roots, could not hold on as the very soil disappeared. Some survived, ironically those of less grandeur than others, and they survived only because they had had less attention from the gardener, and had clung together and grown entwined, and attached themselves more to bedrock than soil.

The gardener could not help but notice that while the plants he had prized most were being destroyed, those he had pain scant attention to, or regarded less, resisted longest. The winds and rain swept over them as it did the rest, and while they suffered certain damage, to a great extent they simply swayed this way and that, as the forces raged over them. Other plants, although full-grown, were still so small in stature that the buffeting passed over them as if they were irrelevant.

Paradoxically, other plants that were new in the garden and still full of potential for growth, were among the first to be washed away when the storm broke.

Other lightning bolts now struck all areas of the garden, striking each of the major trees, either tearing off great limbs or splitting the tree entirely in half.

Everywhere, oaks and firs and even the great gums were left in splintered ruin. Some crashed to earth immediately, others would be left permanently scarred and ugly till they died.

Only the fig remained relatively unscathed. Despite taking the full force of most of the winds, it would not be buckled. Some minor damage was testimony to its inherent solidity, its sureness of being.

As the world disappeared into chaos, the gardener and his wife closed their eyes then, aware that a judgement had been made on them, and that destruction from a far greater Power than that which had been loosed into the garden was exacting revenge.

And as the couple wept together, their tears and blood mingled with the rain and washed over them.

In time, the storm was spent and rolled away.

And as quickly as it had come, it rolled away into the horizon, and left behind a bright, clear sky, and a brilliant new sun seemingly more radiant than the one the couple had remembered from before the storm.

It was over.

The gardener and his wife found the strength to stand, their bodies battered and beaten, and looked over the remnants of what had once been the most majestic garden in the community.

The destruction had been almost total.

The man's body shook with heart-rending sobs that convulsed from deep within him, and burst from him. Waves of grief and anguish flooded over him, purging his soul.

His wife stood in silence behind him. Some part of her wanted to hold him, to console him, but she had neither the will nor the strength to do so.

Inside, she too wept. But wept because of her own failures. She alone had known of her husband's illness and had been powerless to prevent its cancerous spread within him. She had been aware that a cure lay only with the Master they had set out to serve, and His instructions for their lives as so clearly set out in the *Manual*; that only He was able to restore the whole man she had set out on this enterprise with.

She knew, too, that any restoration would be a matter of great pain, if indeed, restoration was possible.

Now, looking upon the devastation before her, wrought upon the very garden she had devoted herself to, she sensed in her spirit that it had been a long time coming.

She wanted to cry alongside her man, but now, no tears would come, just hollowness within. It seemed to her that the rain had scourged not only her flesh, but her very being.

She watched as her husband stepped tentatively into the devastation that had once been his pride and joy.

For his part, the man suddenly realised that with the passing of the storm a clarity of vision had come back to him. The poison in his soul had been cleansed from him, torn from his spirit, and for the first time in a long while, he saw the reality of his foolishness and waywardness. He knew in an instant that his gardening days were done, and it was as if his heart would break completely.

He walked slowly where his prized plants had once stood so grand, where the most treasured specimens had waved at the heavens reflecting his toil and efforts. But they were no more.

Nothing remained in the garden proper. Not that he could see. Except for the fig, the destruction had been complete.

He walked back to his wife who had fallen to her knees, her body racked with tearless sobbing. Gently he knelt beside her, reached out to comfort her, then slowly held her to his chest.

They remained that way for a long time, each in a personal grief beyond the understanding of those who have never dreamed, who have never dared to follow a vision.

Chapter Fourteen

'And this is the judgement,
that the light has come into the world,
and men loved the darkness rather than the light;
for their deeds were evil. For everyone who
does evil hates the light, and does not come into
the light, lest his deeds should be exposed.'

(John 3: 19-20)

The man and his wife stood at the western boundary of the garden that had once been theirs.

They were leaving, and the sadness in their hearts was almost too unbearable for them to carry. With shoulders stooped, they looked for a last time at what they had built, and lost.

The garden was no longer a garden.

Most plants of substance had either been washed away, stripped bare, or lay broken where it had once stood. The great trees stood smouldering, or in embers on the ground. It seemed that none of the trees he had put in place himself, and which had been the source of his greatest pride, had withstood the onslaught.

But here and there, some plants remained intact, clinging precariously to life on isolated patches of sodden soil. Before, the man had long since paid them but scarce attention, but now they were all he had left.

He pointed them out to his wife.

'Survivors,' he remarked.

'Yes, there are always survivors,' said the woman bitterly. 'And having survived this storm, they will be all the stronger next time, should anyone ever garden here again. Perhaps then the gardener will realise that size and boldness of appearance is not necessarily an indication of true worth,' she added in some pain.

'Yet they lack that outward solidity that typifies the best plants,' the man ventured. 'They are plain.'

'And they are still here,' she almost spat the words at him. 'Your 'best' plants are long gone. These ones have deep roots. They have depth, not just show. Don't you understand it yet?'

The man nodded.

He had known it all along. It had been a major error.

'Yes,' he conceded, 'plants of true substance after all.'

They might have been better placed in the garden after all, he admitted to himself.

Everywhere else, he noticed, briars and thorns had sprung up all across the garden expanse, and they stood out prominently in the devastation. Had they always been there, he wondered.

'There is one flower left,' the woman said quietly. 'One solitary flower,' she repeated, pointing to it.

It stood alone, a beautiful bloom of deep, rich white, starkly contrasting with the growth of thistle and thorn and general debris around it.

'It has bloomed despite us,' she said, 'or to spite us.'

The man nodded, looking straight ahead. He didn't want to talk of flowers any more. Not at this time.

'We should be going' he said, instead.

Yes, she thought, he was right. There was neither the need, nor the time to pursue the matter further.

Above them, on a branch of a battered cyprus, six black ravens sat as if to mock the departing couple. They let out a raucous cry that echoed across the valleys.

The man picked up a rock, aimed it at the birds, and threw it at them with all the might he had left.

They mocked him more.

Turning away from the garden, the couple walked from the garden forever, and set out on the road to a new future.

While in the distance, another couple approached the very same area of garden with a spring in their step, and their faces beaming, as if some great promise or inheritance was theirs.

THE END